DERBY MAGIC

Assault, the 1946 Triple Crown champion, in 1951. (Photo courtesy King Ranch Archives, King Ranch, Inc.)

DERBY MAGIC

JIM BOLUS

PELICAN PUBLISHING COMPANY
Gretna 1997

The word "Pelican" and the depiction of a pelican are trademarks
of Pelican Publishing Company, Inc., and are registered
in the U.S. Patent and Trademark Office.

Library of Congress Cataloging-in-Publication Data

Bolus, Jim.
    Derby magic / Jim Bolus.
       p.   cm.
    ISBN 1-56554-276-2 (hc : alk. paper)
    1. Kentucky Derby, Louisville, Ky.—Anecdotes. I. Title.
SF357.K4B625 1997
798.4'009769'44—dc21   96-52479
                                                       CIP

The words "Churchill Downs," "Kentucky Derby," and the repli-
cation of the "Twin Spires" are registered trademarks of Churchill
Downs Incorporated and are used herein with the permission of
Churchill Downs.

Manufactured in the United States of America
Published by Pelican Publishing Company, Inc.
1101 Monroe Street, Gretna, Louisiana 70053

To my father, Eli,

who introduced me to the grand sport of horse racing

Contents

Assault, the 1946 Triple Crown champion, was a focal point for visitors during his retirement at King Ranch in Texas. (Photo courtesy King Ranch Archives, King Ranch, Inc.)

Acknowledgments

For the fifth straight Kentucky Derby book that I have written for Pelican Publishing Company, I first wish to give special thanks to Judy Bortner, director of retail operations for the Kentucky Derby Museum. She suggested my name to Pelican, and since then I have written *Kentucky Derby Stories, Remembering the Derby, Derby Fever, Derby Dreams,* and now *Derby Magic.*

I want to express my sincere gratitude to the devoted people at Pelican for publishing these books. This is a fine publishing company, and it's been a joy for me to work with Pelican on each of these books.

I also wish to acknowledge my indebtedness to Cathy Schenck, head librarian, and assistant Phyllis B. Rogers at the Keeneland Library. Without their help, I would be lost when it comes to researching horse racing in general and the Derby in particular.

I thank the entire staffs at Churchill Downs, notably Tony Terry and Patrick Troutman, and the Kentucky Derby Museum, especially Candace Perry. I am grateful too to Lisa A. Neely, archivist at King Ranch; the University of Kentucky's public relations department; the New York Racing Association press office; the Associated Press; United Press International; and the Louisville Free Public Library.

Books that served as research sources include *Run for the Roses; Boots and Saddles; Whittingham: The Story of a Thoroughbred Racing Legend; Traits of a Winner: The Formula for Developing Thoroughbred Racehorses; Isaac Murphy: Kentucky's Record Jockey; From Here to the Bugle; The Great Ones; The American Turf; Down the Stretch;* and various issues of *The American Racing Manual.*

Numerous publications were used in researching this book, including *The Courier-Journal, Daily Racing Form, The New York Times, Lexington Herald-Leader, The Times-Picayune* (New Orleans), *The Palm Beach Post, The Blood-Horse* magazine,

Thoroughbred Times, the *1988 Kentucky Derby Souvenir Magazine,* the *1990 Kentucky Derby Magazine,* and *The Maryland Horse,* as well as such now-defunct periodicals as *The Louisville Times, The Thoroughbred Record,* the *New York Sun,* and the *New York Daily Running Horse.*

For photographs, I wish to thank Lisa A. Neely, archivist at King Ranch; Stacey Shepherd Yates, communications manager for the Kentucky Derby Festival; Amy Petit at the Keeneland Association; Churchill Downs; the Keeneland Library; the Thoroughbred Racing Associations; the H. E. Sutton Forwarding Co.; Frank L. Jones, Jr.; and the Voice-Tribune.

Hundreds of people have assisted me and been patient with me for many years, and there isn't enough space to list them all. However, I would be remiss if I didn't mention Mike Barry, Don Brumfield, Clay Campbell, Nate Cantrell, Basil Caummisar, Bob Coffey, Frank Coltiletti, John Crittenden, John Cypher, Keene Daingerfield, Pat Day, Ronnie Ebanks, Bert Firestone, Dick Freeman, Vickie Garcia, Willie Garner, Olin Gentry, Cliff Guilliams, Jack Guthrie, Mrs. Howard Y. Haffner, Seth Hancock, Carolyn Hine, Hubert ("Sonny") Hine, Joe Hirsch, J. B. Hitt, Dr. Richard Holder, Pete Johnson, Dr. Gary Lavin, Margaret Layton, Robert Lewis, D. Wayne Lukas, Dan Mangeot, Warren Mehrtens, Mack Miller, Mary Agnes Minton, Ed Musselman, Carl Nafzger, Joe Pierce, Willie Pool, Edwin Pope, J. Morton Porter, Mel Prince, Billy Reed, Richard Stone Reeves, Earl Ruby, Willie ("Smokey") Saunders, Shane Sellers, Whitney Stone, Karen Taylor, Mickey Taylor, Ron Turcotte, John T. Ward, Jr., Charlie Whittingham, and William T. Young.

I also thank *Business First,* in which the "Up, Up, and Away" and Kentucky Derby Festival chapters originally appeared (either entirely or in part).

And, finally, I wish to give my most sincere thanks to Suzanne, my adviser, my typist, my proofreader, my wife since 1964, . . . and the best friend that a person could ever have.

Introduction

The Kentucky Derby is more than a horse race. It's a part of history, an event, a happening. It's all part of the Derby's magic.

What exactly is Derby magic? The written word can't begin to answer that question. The Derby is more than ink on paper. It's an overwhelming spectacle that touches the hearts of those who love the race but leaves them without the proper words to describe its magic.

And there are many of us who do love this old race. In the *1990 Kentucky Derby Magazine,* sports editor Edwin Pope of *The Miami Herald* wrote:

> Kentucky Derby, why loveth I thee so?
>
> I cannot say, but I do. Asking myself why the Derby is my favorite sports event is like asking why my wife is my life. Needing poetry, I can only stammer.
>
> The Derby is, what?
>
> A blur that blinds the eye while binding the soul?
> Yes.
>
> A rush of color and sound and sentiment joined as extravagantly as *Gone With the Wind?* Clangorous as a battlefield? Touching as the Book of Ruth?
> Yes.
>
> In its own way, the Kentucky Derby is all of those to me. Understand this is completely personal. That's part of the magic. I just can't define it.

In the *1988 Kentucky Derby Souvenir Magazine,* executive columnist Joe Hirsch of *Daily Racing Form* wrote:

> What is the mystique of the Kentucky Derby? What makes it the one race that is known the length and breadth of America and beyond? And it is. Confirmation of that status has been cited time and

11

again by those in a position to do so. Charlie Whittingham is one of them. The Dean of Western Trainers, one of the most successful horsemen ever to practice his profession in this country, saddled the winners of hundreds of major races in every section of America. Then, in 1986, at the age of 73, he saddled his first Kentucky Derby winner, Ferdinand.

"I never had the response I received from winning that one race," Whittingham said. "I could win a stakes in California, and a few people might extend congratulations on a casual basis. But everywhere I went after Ferdinand's victory, people wanted to talk about it. I've been in racing all my life, yet I found the reaction amazing."

The Derby is the only race in America that can cause that kind of response. No other racetrack can bottle the Derby's magic. We all know that this magic works at only one track and on only one day of the year: Churchill Downs on the first Saturday in May.

This is my fifth straight Kentucky Derby book published by Pelican Publishing Company. I hope that it touches—just touches—the surface of the Derby's magic. If it does, I'll be happy.

DERBY MAGIC

Don Brumfield. (Photo courtesy Keeneland Association)

1

The Happiest Hillbilly Hardboot

FOR DONALD THOMAS BRUMFIELD, these are happy, busy, bankroll-fattening days at Hialeah Race Course. Blue-eyed, blonde-haired Donald is a trim five-footer. He weighs a bit under a hundred pounds. His father is a horse trainer, and Donald is an apprentice jockey. He's a good one. Take the word of stewards, jockeys, jockey agents, trainers: he's the best apprentice on the premises.

When he arrived in Florida this winter he was dismayed to learn that 17 was the minimum age for a rider here. An appeal was made to the Florida Racing Commission to conform with other states and make it possible for a 16-year-old boy to collect some race-track cash. The commission changed the rule.

The Brumfield horses are in stalls across the way from Sunny Jim Fitzsimmons' barn. One morning last week Mr. Fitz, the 80-year-old dean of the horse trainers, took a look at Don as he was leading a horse around the walking ring. Said Mr. Fitz: "He's a good little boy—and he's a good little rider. He's around here like a boy should be. He's at the barn every morning, doing everything—working horses, walking them, rubbing them, taking care of equipment. He's not a glass-house jockey—by any means."

—James Roach, *The New York Times,*
February 7, 1955

15

Brumfield "has actually been around the stable with his father for nearly eight years, and feels amply ready to step out in his chosen profession," Horace Wade wrote in a 1954 Gulfstream Park publicity release.

> A wee mite of a lad, with short-cropped blond hair, a bridgework of freckles across his nose and a ready smile, he declares that he has yearned to be a rider since he was in the third grade of school. To fulfill this ambition Donald has been walking horses, cleaning stalls, polishing tack and doing the score of menial stable duties since he was eight years old. Asked what weight he can do, Donald replied, "Ninety pounds." That brought an incredulous snort from his father and a confession that: "Eighty-eight is my weight just now."

Brumfield's father, Edgar, a trainer for some thirty-five years, said of Don in 1954, "He has all the earmarks of a rider, plus the will to be one." Don went on to become the all-time leading rider at Churchill Downs and Keeneland. His record 925 victories at the Downs held up until Pat Day broke it in 1990.

Brumfield rode his first race just four days after turning sixteen, in 1954, coming in eighth in a race at Garden State Park. He rode his first winner on August 2, 1954, triumphing with Profizano (trained by his father) in a six-furlong race at Monmouth Park. His first stakes success came aboard Duc de Fer in the Laurel Sprint Handicap on October 30, 1954.

His biggest victory, of course, was the 1966 Kentucky Derby aboard Kauai King. Afterward, the native Kentuckian proclaimed himself "the happiest hillbilly hardboot alive," a quote that will live forever in the race's history.

Mike Ford, the owner of Kauai King, praised Brumfield for "a beautifully judged ride" in the Derby. Brumfield, nicknamed "Boot," rode Kauai King in twelve of his sixteen lifetime starts.

On Derby weekend in 1966, Brumfield also won the Kentucky Oaks with Native Street. He is one of only six

Don Brumfield ranks as the all-time leading rider at Keeneland Race Course in Lexington. (Photo courtesy Keeneland Association by Bill Straus)

jockeys to complete the Oaks-Derby sweep. The other five were Isaac Murphy (1884), Don Meade (1933), Bill Boland (1950), Eddie Arcaro (1952), and Jerry Bailey (1993).

On October 20, 1972, Brumfield established himself as the winningest rider in Keeneland's history. He brought Secret Control home on top in the fourth race for his 234th victorious ride at Keeneland. Fittingly, Secret Control was conditioned by Keeneland's all-time leading trainer at the time, Henry Forrest, who teamed with Brumfield to capture the 1966 Derby with Kauai King.

Before the racing card began the day after his record-breaking win at Keeneland, Brumfield received a julep cup in a paddock presentation honoring him for his feat. Steve Brooks, who held the former record of 233, took part in the ceremony. "Somebody had to break the record," he said. "I can't think of anyone I would rather see do it than Don. We have been friends for many years."

Brumfield rode thirty winners at Keeneland in the spring of '74, a record at the time. Two of his triumphs came in the divisions of the Ashland Stakes. But don't think for a moment that he had to deliberate about which of the victorious fillies—Winged Wishes or Maud Muller—he planned to ride back in the Kentucky Oaks. The jockey's mother, Viola Brumfield, owned Winged Wishes, and Don himself bred the filly, so it went without saying which horse he'd ride in the Oaks. As a beaming Brumfield put it after scoring his Ashland sweep, "I'd have to ride her [Winged Wishes] back or my mother would break my supper dish."

Brumfield said his mother gave him just brief instructions before Winged Wishes' division of the Ashland. "She said, 'Hurry home,'" Don related with a smile. Brumfield got home as fast as he could, driving Winged Wishes to a 1½-length victory.

In the Oaks, Brumfield rode Winged Wishes to a fourth-place finish, while Maud Muller was thirteenth in the field of fourteen.

Don Brumfield was a favorite with fans and writers during his highly successful riding career. "The secret to longevity of 'The Boot' is his discipline, more than anything," Billy Reed wrote in The Courier-Journal *in 1982. "Brumfield has never had a serious weight problem because he refuses to overindulge on food, even the fish that he has come to love. He's the sort of guy who has taken excellent care of his mother, Viola, who lives in Lexington. A loyal person, a good person. His description of his father—'A man who wouldn't take any bull from anybody, but who wouldn't give any, either'—also applies to Don Brumfield at age 44."*
(Photo courtesy Churchill Downs)

Brumfield remains Keeneland's all-time leading jockey in total victories, with 716. He was the top Keeneland rider at a record sixteen meetings—the spring of 1972, 1973, 1974, 1975, 1976, 1979, and 1984 and the fall of 1964, 1967, 1969, 1971, 1972, 1973, 1974, 1975 (a tie), and 1980.

On May 24, 1988, Brumfield's fiftieth birthday, the veteran jockey was honored in a ceremony in the Churchill Downs paddock. Brumfield, who rode his first winner at the Downs on October 27, 1956, was quite popular with the fans, some of whom were known to yell, "Sweep 'em, Broom" as he rode a horse to the lead at the head of the stretch.

Brumfield rode his last race on September 16, 1989 at Turfway Park, finishing fourth on Batim in the Alysheba Stakes. "I'm fifty-one, and it's kind of hard to keep competing with the younger kids," he said at the time. "If I don't satisfy myself riding, I don't think I can satisfy anyone else."

He retired as the fourteenth-leading jockey on the all-time list, with 4,572 victories to his credit. He also had 4,076 seconds and 3,759 thirds from 33,222 mounts and purse earnings of $43,557,499. The numbers tell only part of his story, not taking into account "his untold influence on young riders, so many of whom would scrutinize his style and try to emulate his left-hand whip," wrote *The Courier-Journal's* Jennie Rees.

Setting out on a new career as a racing official, Brumfield became a patrol judge at Keeneland's 1989 fall meeting. During his retirement, he also has served as a jockey's agent.

For his achievements as a jockey, Brumfield was honored by being inducted into racing's Hall of Fame on August 5, 1996. "I never thought I'd be in the Hall of Fame because I never thought I was that kind of person," he said. "Winning the Derby was the most special day in my life, and this has got to be right up there behind it. This is what you work your entire life for."

> Long after his numbers are forgotten, Brumfield will be remembered for his honesty and his competitive spirit. Horsemen and bettors alike knew that when

Don Brumfield (sunglasses) was honored by track president Tom Meeker and jockeys and valets at Churchill Downs in a 1996 awards ceremony recognizing his election into racing's Hall of Fame. (Photo courtesy Churchill Downs)

"Boot" was in the saddle, they might not always get a winner, but they would never get less than 100 percent. He was an honest workman who was known for his ability to get home with 2-year-olds, especially at Keeneland and Churchill, and for his meaningful use of the whip.

It's almost unimaginable that we'll be able to go to Keeneland or Churchill and not see Brumfield's name in the program as a jockey. In his own quiet way, for an incredibly long period, he has embodied the essence of his profession—the character and courage that belong to only the winners.

So goodbye, Don, and thanks. You gave us your best, always, and rest assured that we'll always have a special respect for the happiest hillbilly hardboot in the world.

—Billy Reed, *Lexington Herald-Leader,*
September 29, 1989

William T. Young with jockey Chris McCarron following Corporate Report's victory in the 1991 Travers. (Photo by Jim Bolus)

2

William T. Young—
a Revered Kentuckian

FOR WILLIAM T. YOUNG, 1996 was a year that came up roses. Grindstone, bred and owned by Young's Overbrook Farm, provided this distinguished Kentuckian with the ultimate thrill in racing. On May 4, he came through with an electrifying finish, winning the Kentucky Derby by a nose in the last stride.

In the post-Derby press conference, Young said, "It was a great moment; you know how I feel. You are all writers—use your own adjectives. I'll endorse any good adjectives you come up with."

Although Grindstone was retired with an injury after the Derby, Young came back on June 8 to win the Belmont Stakes, the third leg in the Triple Crown, with Editor's Note. After the Belmont, Young commented on winning two legs of the Triple Crown that year. "Words are hard to come by," he said. "You can't add much to a superlative. This is a scenario you only dream of. We have a sound horse here. This may be the first good older-horse prospect we've had in a while; that's exciting. The furthest thing from my mind is to win another Derby or Belmont. It's just asking too much. This has been a tremendous thrill.

"If I hadn't been born in Lexington, I would not be in the horse business," Young added. "I've associated myself with the finest trainer there is, and I've felt that way for ten years."

Young's trainer is D. Wayne Lukas, who lauds the owner for the effect that he has on people. "As we go through life," Lukas said, "each of us cross paths with many, many different people. But every once in a while, you cross paths with somebody who really makes a difference. Bill Young is that type of person. It seems that every time he touches somebody's life, they're better for it. That has certainly been the case with me and I'm sure countless others. He is one of these people who makes everybody around him better. I've been blessed to have a long association with him in the horse business, but as I have gotten to know him more and more, I realize that he also has that effect on many, many other people's lives who are outside of the horse business and in the state of Kentucky."

Besides winning the 1996 Kentucky Derby and Belmont, Young has enjoyed many other big moments in racing. He won the 1990 Kentucky Oaks with Seaside Attraction and the 1991 Travers with Corporate Report, whom he owned in partnership with Lukas. Young and partner David P. Reynolds raced Tabasco Cat, the 1994 Preakness and Belmont winner. He also was a part owner of another classic winner—Timber Country, who captured the 1994 Breeders' Cup Juvenile and the 1995 Preakness. And in 1996 he owned Boston Harbor, winner of the Breeders' Cup Juvenile at Woodbine.

Timber Country was voted champion two-year-old colt of 1994. Flanders and Golden Attraction, both bred and owned by Young, won the Eclipse Award as champion two-year-old filly of 1994 and 1995, respectively. And Boston Harbor, owned and bred by Overbrook, was honored as champion two-year-old colt of 1996.

Young owned his first Thoroughbreds in the 1970s and began a steady climb to the top echelon of breeding and racing in the 1980s.

At Overbrook Farm, a 1,600-acre spread in Lexington, the following seven stallions stood the 1996 breeding season:

A beaming William T. Young received the trophy from D. G. Van Clief, Jr., executive director of the Breeders' Cup, following Boston Harbor's victory in the 1996 Breeders' Cup Juvenile at Woodbine. (Photo by Jim Bolus)

William T. Young held the Eclipse Award that was presented to his Golden Attraction, the champion two-year-old filly of 1995. (Photo courtesy Richard Boardman)

Boone's Mill, Carson City, Corporate Report, Deposit Ticket, Mountain Cat, Storm Cat, and Tabasco Cat.

Storm Cat, one of the most sought after sires in America, was Young's first major stakes competitor. In 1985, he won the Young America and finished second, losing by just a nose, in the Breeders' Cup Juvenile. Storm Cat won four of eight starts in an abbreviated career. "Looking back, I always felt he probably should have been undefeated," Young said. "He had such a will to win that even in workouts he just wouldn't let a horse get past him."

Young, born February 15, 1918, was educated in Lexington public schools and graduated in 1939 from the University of Kentucky with high distinction in mechanical engineering. After World War II, he founded W. T. Young Foods, in Lexington, to manufacture Big Top peanut butter. The business was expanded to national distribution, and in 1955 Young sold the company to Procter & Gamble, which renamed the brand Jif. He headed that subsidiary for Procter & Gamble until 1957.

In 1958, he founded W. T. Young Storage, a trucking and storage company that is now run by his son, William T. Young, Jr.

The elder Young was chairman of Royal Crown Cola Company from 1966 until the company was sold in the mid-1980s. He and Lucy, his wife since the 1940s, have another child—Lucy, who was married to the late French trainer François Boutin.

From 1979 to 1981, Young was vice-chairman of the Kentucky cabinet under Gov. John Y. Brown, Jr. He has been active in civic and educational matters, serving as a major benefactor and board chairman of Transylvania University. He has been a significant contributor to the University of Kentucky for its new library, which will bear his name. His donation of $5 million was the largest cash gift ever made to UK by an alumnus. "The best years of my life were spent at the University of Kentucky," Young said.

A director emeritus at Churchill Downs, he was elected to The Jockey Club in 1989. Young received the 1994 Eclipse Award as outstanding breeder in North America. For the year, he bred or cobred fourteen stakes winners.

In 1996, he was inducted into the Kentucky Athletic Hall of Fame and was the guest of honor at the Lexington-based Thoroughbred Club of America's prestigious testimonial dinner.

In a 1996 *Daily Racing Form* column headlined "Through good and bad, Young still the same," Cliff Guilliams wrote:

> When his Union City broke down in the 1993 Preakness, several media vultures wanted Lukas with a

William T. Young (left) received the Eclipse Award for outstanding breeder of 1994 from James E. ("Ted") Bassett III, president of the Breeders' Cup and board chairman of the Keeneland Association. (Photo courtesy Cappy Jackson)

rope around his neck and fired off unfounded claims in print. It was Young who stepped from behind the curtain and informed the media that it was his decision to run Union City, not the trainer's.

And, when Flanders broke down while winning the Breeders' Cup Juvenile Fillies, or the gallant dual classic-winning Tabasco Cat retired, Young never whimpered, hung his head or looked for sympathy. He's fully aware of the risks taken in the big arena and referred to their grit under fire, saying: "Look how much we've been blessed with."

It was virtually the same story last May when Grindstone departed center stage with a bone chip in a knee a week after he won the Derby. Did Young bemoan the fact or hedge on further surgery? Never. He said typically: "We had our day in the sun. He's retired and hopefully will make a great sire."

William T. Young well deserves his standing as a revered Kentuckian and a nationally known figure in American Thoroughbred racing.

3

It Doesn't Get Any Better
Than D. Wayne Lukas

THERE IS NO SECRET to trainer D. Wayne Lukas's success story. He does his job the old-fashioned way: he works at it. Every morning—I mean *every* morning, including Christmas and all other holidays—he awakens between 3:00 and 3:30 to start his day. He arrives at the barn by 4:00 to begin work. In his stables in Kentucky and California are boards that spell out *The Trainer's Daily Dozen*—lessons that all of us could take through life to make the most of each day. It is made up of the following: the value of time, the success of perseverance, the pleasure of working, the dignity of simplicity, the worth of character, the power of kindness, the influence of example, the obligation of duty, the wisdom of economy, the virtue of patience, the improvement of talent, and the joy of originating.

Even while attending a horse sale, he arises that early and checks by telephone with the various divisions of his stable. Normally he has three divisions in different parts of the country. During the course of 1996, he averaged 125 horses in his care.

On off days at tracks where he's stabled, you won't find him playing golf in the afternoons. No, he arrives at the track at that time and personally helps graze his horses.

Lukas has worked hard all his life. A graduate of the University of Wisconsin—Madison, he coached basketball two years at Blair High School in that state. He returned to

the university as an assistant basketball coach for two seasons and then spent the next seven years (1960-61 through
1966-67) as head coach at Logan High School in La Crosse.

When he left basketball for a career as a trainer, it was
horse racing's gain. Lukas already has trained nineteen
North American champions and thirteen winners of
Breeders' Cup Championship races, both records. He has
ranked as the country's leading money-winning trainer for

*D. Wayne Lukas, trainer of a record nineteen North American
champions, received the Eclipse Award for Flanders' two-year-old-filly title
in 1994. Presenting the trophy at the Eclipse Awards Dinner in
Washington, D.C., was John Nash, general manager of the Washington
Bullets professional basketball team. (Photo courtesy Cappy Jackson)*

thirteen years (1983 through 1992 and then again in 1994, 1995, and 1996). He has won the Eclipse Award as outstanding trainer four times—1985, 1986, 1987, and 1994.

He has trained three Kentucky Derby winners—Winning Colors (a filly) in 1988, Thunder Gulch in 1995, and Grindstone in 1996. In 1995, he became the first trainer ever to win all three Triple Crown races with two different horses—the Derby and Belmont with Thunder Gulch and the Preakness with Timber Country. Those three successes came on the heels of victories in the final two legs of the 1994 Triple Crown series, the Preakness and Belmont with Tabasco Cat.

Grindstone, who was considered no better than a third stringer among the five 1996 Derby starters sent out by Lukas, came through with a furious finish to win the 122nd Derby. Two of Lukas's 1996 Derby starters ran in entries— Grindstone and Editor's Note forming a twosome and Victory Speech and Honour and Glory coupled in another. Prince of Thieves, who ran as a separate betting interest, was the other Lukas starter.

Among the Lukas horses, Grindstone would have been ranked behind Editor's Note and Prince of Thieves and ahead of Victory Speech and Honour and Glory. In 1995, Lukas also won the Derby with a third stringer, Thunder Gulch, who was ranked behind Timber Country and Serena's Song among the trainer's three starters in the race.

Grindstone came into the Derby with only five starts under his belt. Earlier in the year, he had been sent by Lukas to run in the Louisiana Derby, which he won, and the Arkansas Derby, in which he ran second. In the Kentucky Derby, Grindstone received a brilliant ride from Jerry Bailey, who weaved the colt from far back in the field of nineteen. Charging on the outside, Grindstone overtook Cavonnier in the final stride to win by a nose in one of the most electrifying finishes in Derby history. The Derby was Lukas's unprecedented sixth straight victory in a Triple Crown race.

Lukas was criticized by some people for starting five horses in the Derby, a record for the race. In their previous starts, all five had finished in the money and four had been favored, although none of them had won. Still, it was obvious that they belonged in the Derby. Indeed, Lukas-trained horses finished first (Grindstone), third (Prince of Thieves), and sixth (Editor's Note). His other two starters ran tenth (Victory Speech) and eighteenth (Honour and Glory). Honour and Glory didn't figure to go the Derby distance, but he had enough quality to belong in the race. He demonstrated that quality by winning the Metropolitan Handicap twenty-three days after the Derby. As for Victory Speech, later in the 1996 season he won such major races as the Dwyer Stakes and Swaps Stakes.

Lukas's streak in Triple Crown races ended in the 1996 Preakness, but he came back to win the Belmont with Editor's Note. In this incredible Triple Crown run, Lukas triumphed in seven of these eight classics—and with five different horses, quite a feat.

Winning the Preakness and Belmont with Tabasco Cat in 1994 underlined Lukas's tremendous training ability.

Following Tabasco Cat's disappointing sixth-place finish in the Kentucky Derby, Lukas helped the colt get his act together for the Preakness. "Going into the Derby," the trainer said, "with the schedule I had him on, I think I had him physically fit. In hindsight, he might have been just a hair too sharp, although I'm not sure of that."

Mentally, Tabasco Cat always had been "a little more aggressive than you'd want a horse that's going to run classic distances to be," Lukas added. "So between the Derby and the Preakness, I tried to relax him and take a little off his fastball, bring him back a little bit. I tried to spend a little bit more time with him one on one." Lukas kept Tabasco Cat out for longer grazes, and "I walked him a little bit longer; I tacked him up and left him tacked a little bit longer."

He continued his training pattern with Tabasco Cat between the Preakness and the Belmont. He also let the colt play in the sand at Belmont Park. "I put him in that sand pen and let him roll and frolic in there for forty-five minutes every day," Lukas said. "There's a certain amount of risk doing that because they get to playing pretty hard. Of course, he was a dead-fit horse so he played *very* hard. But it helped settle him every day."

Jockey Pat Day was among those praising Lukas for the job that he did with Tabasco Cat. "Wayne deserves a real pat on the back," Day said at the time. "He spent a lot of time with that horse. He got right between that horse's ears. He watched him, studied him, knew everything about him, knew him intimately. It was through that time that he spent with him that he learned what it took to make the horse happy and ultimately to get him to go a mile and a half."

In addition to being a hard worker, Lukas is a superb organizer. He believes in taking care of every detail in the operation of his stable. His barns are immaculate, and his horses always are given the best of care. With so many horses spread across the country, he is a great manager.

Lukas believes in himself. He does things his way. While many trainers shy away from running fillies against colts, Lukas won the 1988 Derby with the filly Winning Colors. He has run fillies against colts on other occasions, including triumphs by Serena's Song in the 1995 Jim Beam Stakes and Haskell Invitational Handicap.

There are some coaches of athletic teams who coach not to lose instead of coaching to win. Lukas doesn't train not to lose. He trains to win, which is evidence of his confidence. He is a master planner, mapping out a schedule for his horses well in advance. He doesn't leave anything to chance.

All of this hard work and planning has paid off in a big way. Simply put, no trainer in the history of the sport has produced the way Lukas has—purse winnings, champions, consecutive winners of Triple Crown races, Breeders' Cup

Championship winners. *Daily Racing Form*'s Cliff Guilliams, one of Lukas's biggest supporters in the media, wrote the following in a June 18, 1995 column:

> Perhaps Pierre "Peb" Bellocq, *Daily Racing Form*'s art director, described it best with colored ink.
>
> On the front page of last Saturday's editions, Peb penned a wonderful caricature of trainer D. Wayne Lukas driving a chariot around an arena that was supposed to resemble the Colosseum of ancient Rome. Lukas, standing in the cart adorned in plumed helmet and complete battle regalia, was driving, of course, the team of Timber Country and Thunder Gulch.
>
> Perhaps this was a sign of things to come because ABC-TV baited Lukas into mugging on camera for the Belmont telecast. Mugging is totally out of character for this great trainer.
>
> Topping off Lukas' uniform was a flowing red cape.
>
> "You can compare Lukas to Caesar, now," someone said. "Caesar wore a red tunic and cape in battle to distinguish him from his men, same as Peb put on Lukas."
>
> This is true and there are more similarities.
>
> Caesar was not, and Lukas is not, lovable. Yet, both were generous with praise to vanquished opponents and are deeply admired and respected for it. For example, the first person Lukas saluted was Nick Zito, who has trained numerous runner-ups during Lukas' "drive for five."
>
> Lukas, like Caesar, won the approval and devotion of his fans by one simple item: winning. It was through victories brought about by his intelligence applied to training horses and having them at their peak for important races that have given Lukas a place in history.

In early 1996, I asked two Lukas clients, William T. Young and Robert Lewis, to provide some insight into the trainer's success. Young, the Overbrook Farm master, offered these remarks.

In thinking about your request for my observations on Wayne Lukas, I was first tempted to comment on some of his more notable horses and his remarkable success as a trainer. However, it occurred to me that others could speak to these issues and much has already been said and written. Accordingly, I thought I would address some of the less visible "behind the scenes" things, which, while perhaps mundane, contribute greatly to Wayne's success. Specifically, I think much of his success can be attributed to three strengths: his indefatigable work ethic, his knack for finding outstanding assistants, and his remarkable horsemanship.

First, as to his work ethic, Wayne, like most successful people, is a workaholic. Because I reside in the Eastern time zone and am an early riser myself, I often call him at Santa Anita at 4:00 A.M. his time. He is always there when I call, and he puts in incredibly long days. In the years he has been my trainer, I am not aware of a single vacation day he has taken. He works seven days a week. The days Santa Anita is dark, you will often find Wayne at his training center at Westerly [California]. He is also one of the most intense people I have known, so that he doesn't just put in the time, but his time spent is normally productive.

The second thing I admire about Wayne is his ability to attract some of the most talented assistants in the business. However, I can recall some press suggesting that the departure of some of his top people was symptomatic of other problems that were contributing to a prolonged losing streak at the track. Top assistants like Randy Bradshaw, Mark Hennig, and Kiaran McLaughlin were moving out on their own. I remember thinking at the time that those who were criticizing Wayne were completely missing the boat. The very thing they were criticizing was in fact a source of his strength. It would be like criticizing Rick Pitino because he lost Billy Donovan, Tubby Smith, Ralph Willard, and Herb Sendek, who all left for greener pastures. It is the very nature of good people that they

eventually will leave to be on their own, whether the
field is horse racing or basketball. Today, Wayne's
organization is still staffed by top young horsemen,
who, like their predecessors, will ultimately graduate
to become successful trainers in their own right.

The third thing I would mention is his unques-
tioned horsemanship. Wayne's horses may not win all
the races, but they always win the paddock show, and
Wayne personally handles the most spirited horses. To
this day, I am convinced Wayne's personal handling of
Tabasco Cat is the primary reason the colt won two
legs of the Triple Crown. Speaking of Tabasco Cat, I
can recall after he was retired from racing the day he
arrived at Overbrook to begin his stallion duties.
Tabasco Cat's routine that day had been disturbed by a
two-hour morning van ride, and he was greeted at
Overbrook by about a hundred people, including the
media with all their cameras and paraphernalia. Always
full of fire, Tabasco Cat understandably was jittery
from all this activity. Undeterred, Wayne calmly took
the shank and paraded the excited horse back and
forth for about fifteen minutes. Once, when Tabasco
Cat reared up, his leg came down across the shank.
Those in the crowd who saw what happened gasped in
fear the horse would bolt free. However, Wayne, the
consummate horseman, in a split second, dropped the
shank from the "trapped" hand and grasped it above
the stallion's leg with the other hand. Most in the
crowd never knew what happened, but Wayne's horsemanship saved the day.

Lewis, who races horses with his wife, Beverly, commented
on Lukas's personality, saying, "What has become very evident is his humanness and emotional understanding of
other people's needs or desires. I have found Wayne to be
very sympathetic when placed in a one-on-one situation. I
believe that the media oftentimes gets the wrong impression
because of his ability to answer questions in a manner that is
very direct and, for that reason, can be misconstrued. Wayne

truly feels that the horse must come first and that, if you properly read the makeup of the horse and the signals that the horse is attempting to convey, you can best understand his needs.

"I think Wayne learned this from his early days in coaching and teaching youngsters the game of basketball. Wayne has told me stories of that period of his life, of the need for understanding, and of his attempts to diagnose what young men really needed in their athletic endeavors.

"These characteristics of Wayne were very evident when he spoke recently to a dinner group of over three hundred people and related the thoughts that came to his mind during Jeff's rehabilitation period," Lewis added, referring to the recovery of Wayne's son following life-threatening head injuries suffered when he was run over by Tabasco Cat in the Santa Anita Park stable area on December 15, 1993. "Wayne became, understandably, quite emotional, and those who were in attendance saw the other side of D. Wayne Lukas. He is truly a sensitive person who is genuinely concerned with those he comes in contact with.

"A person who has seen this side of Wayne is [trainer] Brian Mayberry, who holds Wayne in the very highest regard. He has seen the sensitive and compassionate side of this basketball coach who has become one of the country's leading Thoroughbred trainers. Beverly and I have found that he is an excellent teacher, as his educational background qualifies him for. The Lukas organization runs like clockwork. He keeps us extremely well informed as one of his clients and seems genuinely interested in his clients' satisfaction and rewards. He runs an organization that strives for excellence, and he constantly conveys this message to all of his personnel. They seem to react with a sense of pride in that they are among the very best and they know it."

A man doesn't train nineteen champions without being a superb horseman, and Lukas ranks among the greatest trainers of all time. His record simply speaks for itself. Among

Lukas's nineteen champions have been two Horses of the Year—Lady's Secret in 1986 and Criminal Type in 1990.

While many other men his age are beginning to think about retirement, Lukas is looking ahead to continued successes on the racetrack. "We're in the zone again," Lukas told sportswriter Billy Reed in 1995 with a smile and a wink, "and I don't see why our next ten years can't be our best years."

Lukas has come a long way from his early years as a horseman, days spent on dusty tracks in places far away from the glamor of Keeneland and Churchill Downs, Santa Anita Park and Belmont Park. He has an interesting background as a horseman. He taught himself everything he knows. He purchased and sold horses at auction when he was just eight or nine years old. As a youngster, he listened to the old-time horsemen at the Antigo County (Wisconsin) fairgrounds and "picked their brains, sitting around in the evenings." But he never worked as an assistant trainer. He has developed his ideas and methods strictly on his own.

He trained quarter horses and some Thoroughbreds in his early years. He was the leading quarter-horse trainer in money won in 1974, 1975, and 1976 and in races won in 1970, 1974, and 1975. Lukas turned to Thoroughbreds on a full-time basis in 1978, but it should be noted that he had trained that breed for more than ten years before then.

Since entering the Thoroughbred industry, Lukas has carved out a record that may never be equaled. He has won virtually every major stakes race in the country. His Team Lukas operation has achieved a standard of excellence unparalleled in the history of the sport.

A horseman with a sharp eye for yearlings, Lukas has acquired many outstanding horses at auction. He has spent millions of dollars at Keeneland sales. Acting on behalf of a four-man American syndicate made up of himself, Bob French, Eugene Klein, and Mel Hatley, he was the underbidder on the world-record $13.1-million yearling that sold at Keeneland in 1985. He has had particularly good success purchasing horses at Keeneland, including the following seven champions:

1. Capote—1985 July sale, $800,000
2. Landaluce—1981 July sale, $650,000
3. Life's Magic—1982 September sale, $310,000
4. Sacahuista—1985 July sale, $670,000
5. Serena's Song—1993 July sale, $150,000

D. Wayne Lukas (right) was honored with the Warner L. Jones, Jr. Horseman of the Year Award in 1995 at the Kentucky Derby Museum. The Kentucky Thoroughbred Owners, primarily Churchill Downs-based owners, presented the award. Frank L. Jones, Jr., president of the Kentucky Thoroughbred Owners, and Mrs. Warner L. Jones, Jr., are shown with Lukas at the 1995 function. (Photo courtesy Voice-Tribune)

6. Timber Country—1993 July sale, $500,000
7. Winning Colors—1987 July sale, $575,000

Recalling his opinion of Winning Colors at the sale, Lukas once said, "She had it all. When she walked out, I went around her about twice and I didn't want to draw a lot of attention. I said, 'Put her away.' It's like when Liz Taylor walks in a room, you don't have to have everybody tell you that's a pretty woman."

Besides these champions, Lukas has trained such other outstanding Keeneland sales products as 1985 Preakness winner Tank's Prospect ($625,000), 1991 Travers winner Corporate Report ($350,000), Blush With Pride ($650,000), Marfa ($300,000), Terlingua ($275,000), Pancho Villa ($1.8 million), Grand Canyon ($825,000), Is It True ($550,000), Hennessy ($500,000), and Miraloma ($335,000).

Lukas's purchase of Serena's Song proved to be quite a bargain. She finished her career with earnings of $3,283,388, a record for a North American female racehorse. That's not a bad return on a $150,000 investment. Serena's Song is one of many examples of her trainer's expertise. When it comes to buying yearlings and training racehorses, nobody does it any better than D. Wayne Lukas.

D. Wayne Lukas's Champions

Althea—2-year-old filly, 1983
Boston Harbor—2-year-old colt, 1996
Capote—2-year-old colt, 1986
Criminal Type—older male and Horse of the Year, 1990
Family Style—2-year-old filly, 1985
Flanders—2-year-old filly, 1994
Golden Attraction—2-year-old filly, 1995
Gulch—sprinter, 1988
Lady's Secret—older filly or mare and Horse of the Year, 1986
Landaluce—2-year-old filly, 1982

Life's Magic—3-year-old filly, 1984; older filly or mare, 1985

North Sider—older filly or mare, 1987

Open Mind—2-year-old filly, 1988; 3-year-old filly, 1989

Sacahuista—3-year-old filly, 1987

Serena's Song—3-year-old filly, 1995

Steinlen—male grass horse, 1989

Thunder Gulch—3-year-old colt, 1995

Timber Country—2-year-old colt, 1994

Winning Colors—3-year-old filly, 1988

Charlie Whittingham, "the Bald Eagle." (Photo by Jim Bolus)

4

The Bull and the Sunshine Boys

THEY WERE CALLED the "Sunshine Boys," and the sun has never shone more brightly on any old-timers at historic Churchill Downs than it did on those two gentlemen at the 1986 Kentucky Derby. Charlie Whittingham and Bill Shoemaker made history in that Derby when they teamed to win the roses with a rangy colt by the name of Ferdinand. At seventy-three, Whittingham became the oldest trainer ever to win the Derby, and at fifty-four Shoemaker became the oldest jockey to triumph in this classic.

It was a very good year for sports veterans in 1986. The month before the Derby, Jack Nicklaus won the Masters Golf Tournament at the age of forty-six. But not many people expected Whittingham and Shoemaker to pull off their Derby victory with Ferdinand, a colt who was well bred but hadn't accomplished all that much on the racetrack.

Ferdinand, sired by 1970 English Triple Crown champion Nijinsky II, was foaled at Claiborne Farm, near Paris, Kentucky. This chestnut colt was bred by Howard Keck and raced for his wife, Elizabeth.

Nijinsky II's offspring had shown a definite liking for grass, but turf racing didn't prove to be Ferdinand's cup of tea. In the summer of Ferdinand's four-year-old season, Mrs. Keck provided this explanation for the colt's name: "Mr. Keck brought back from Africa a green soapstone sculpture of a bull done by a black man who is a very talented sculptor.

Since it didn't fit anyplace in the house, I kept moving him around from spot to spot and finally found a home for him on Mr. Keck's bookshelf. During this process, we fondly nicknamed the sculpture 'Ferdinand.'"

For years she had spent considerable time naming their horses, but in this particular case she and Mr. Keck "decided, in some merriment, to name the colt Ferdinand, perhaps because he reminded us of the bull who loved to smell the flowers, which in his case is a joke as he hates the grass!" Mrs. Keck explained. "I am afraid that he has found out that grass is only for eating purposes and not for running."

Ferdinand wasn't exactly tearing up the racing world on the dirt early in his career. Under the patient handling of Whittingham, the colt came around and developed into a champion. But at the time of the Derby he had just two victories under his belt in nine starts. In his final Derby prep, he finished third, trailing the triumphant Snow Chief by seven lengths in the Santa Anita Derby. Whittingham, undismayed, made travel plans for Louisville. "He can't handle a slick racetrack," the trainer said. "But if the track at Churchill Downs is good and firm, he's going to do just fine."

The mere presence of Whittingham at Churchill Downs should have told observers plenty about Ferdinand's chances in the Derby. "The Bald Eagle" had trained two previous Derby starters—Gone Fishin' in 1958 and Divine Comedy in 1960, long shots who finished far back. Afterward, Whittingham wasn't interested in making the trip to Louisville unless he thought his horse belonged in the Derby.

In 1954, Whittingham had a serious Derby candidate in Porterhouse, but bruised hooves sidelined this future-book favorite. For a quarter of a century before 1986, Whittingham trained other three-year-old prospects—Eagle Admiral (1960) and Perfect Sky (1965), Saber Mountain (1966) and Tumble Wind (1967), Quack (1972) and Balzac (1978). But something always seemed to go wrong on the road to

Louisville—an injury or a horse wasn't even nominated to the Derby—or Whittingham decided against making the trip in the best interest of the horse.

Now in 1986 Whittingham was headed to Churchill Downs with only his third Derby starter in his Hall of Fame career. "Whittingham has always regarded Ferdinand as the best 3-year-old candidate he's trained in years," *Daily Racing Form*'s Joe Hirsch wrote before the colt left California. "The big chestnut colt has had his moments, but has knocked on the door of opportunity more often than he opened it."

Ferdinand was shipped to Louisville on April 18 and proceeded to train well over the racetrack. He worked twice at the Downs, both times with undefeated stablemate Hidden Light. In both workouts, exercise rider Larry Gilligan was up on Ferdinand and Shoemaker was aboard Hidden Light, a three-year-old filly. Ferdinand wasn't a good work horse, and Whittingham figured that training him with Hidden Light might keep him interested. On April 24, Ferdinand went a mile in an outstanding 1:38⅘, and five days later he ran five furlongs in 58⅗ seconds. In the latter workout, Hidden Light broke off three lengths in front.

"When I asked him to run," Gilligan said of the April 29 workout, "he motored right to her." And instead of easing himself up, he charged past her in an impressive move. "There is no question he seems to like this track," Whittingham said after that workout. "He also seems to be coming to hand as an individual. There is enough speed in this Derby to make his stretch run effective, if Ferdinand has a little racing luck, and he has a rider who has been there before. The game is on."

The mile workout didn't help Hidden Light's chances in the Kentucky Oaks, a race in which Mrs. Keck's filly would finish seventh. Indeed, that particular workout with Ferdinand "took a lot out of her," Whittingham recalled in a recent interview. "She wasn't as sharp for the Oaks as she would have been. I said, 'Well, sacrifice one for the other.'"

Shoemaker had ridden three previous Derby winners—
Swaps in 1955, Tomy Lee in 1959, and Lucky Debonair in
1965. Only five of the other fifteen riders in the Derby were
living when Shoemaker won his first race in 1949. The
youngest jockeys in that Derby were Keith Allen, twenty-one;
Alex Solis, twenty-two; and Gary Stevens, twenty-three.

At an age when most jockeys are retired, Shoemaker was
still going strong in the 1980s. In 1980, he rode the great
Spectacular Bid to Horse of the Year honors. The next year
he rode the rallying John Henry to an electrifying victory
over The Bart in the inaugural Arlington Million.
Shoemaker won the Del Mar Handicap two straight years—
aboard Muttering in 1982 and Bel Bolide in 1983. In 1985,
Shoemaker and Whittingham combined to capture the
Santa Anita Handicap with Lord At War.

But even though he was still winning races, Shoemaker
was fifty-four years old in 1986, and some cynics wondered
whether, at his age, he would enhance or hurt Ferdinand's
chances in the Derby. Would Shoemaker be daring enough
to go through the inside in a big field or would he, as some
suggested, prefer the safer overland route? And, at his age,
what about his reflexes? In short, was the Shoe washed up?
The veteran jockey was prepared to answer the doubters on
Derby Day.

A crowd of 123,819 turned out for the 112th Derby, in-
cluding such celebrities as Gerald Ford, Tom Brokaw, Don
Johnson, Susan Lucci, Ginger Rogers, Gary Collins, and
Ricky Skaggs.

From a record 452 nominees, 16 went to the post for the
Derby. Snow Chief was favored at 2.10-1. Listed at 20-1 in
the program's morning line, Ferdinand went off at 17-1.
The *Louisville Daily Sports News,* popularly known around
town as "the finger sheet," picked Ferdinand to win.
Looking into a crystal ball, astute handicapper Don DeWitt
made this observation about Ferdinand: "Strong as a bull in
the final quarter-mile."

Soon after breaking from his number-one post position, Ferdinand found himself in trouble. "It's always tight coming out of the number-one post, and I got pinched back further than I wanted to be," Shoemaker would say later. "I had to pull the horse back. He was as close as he could get to the rail without going over. Then he kind of checked himself. He knew he was close. But then he started running nicely."

Ferdinand, who dropped back to last the first time he passed the finish line, began making up some ground going down the backstretch. Then, from the half-mile pole to the quarter pole, he launched a big move to reach a contending position. In the upper stretch, Shoemaker had to make a quick decision—whether to go around three horses or through a hole. Shoemaker shot through the hole. Somebody later asked him, "Wasn't that dangerous?"

"You don't think about that in the Kentucky Derby," Shoemaker said.

How much time did Shoemaker have to make that decision? "About three seconds," he replied. "I said, 'Well, I'm going to take a chance and save ground; it might make a difference.' He shot through the hole. When you have enough horse, you can go through those holes." Shoemaker had more than enough horse, and Ferdinand charged through the opening like a bolt of lightning.

The Churchill Downs stretch is a long one, but the 1¼-mile Derby has a way of separating the men from the boys well before the finish line. Generally, the horse who leads at the eighth pole will wind up with the roses. Forget the fact that Ferdinand liked to loaf once he gained the lead. He was rolling now, on his way to victory. "Here comes *Ferdinand* on the rail!" exclaimed track announcer Mike Battaglia as the field neared the eighth pole. There was still a furlong left in the Derby, but Ferdinand was in front and the horses behind him weren't about to overtake him. This Derby belonged to Ferdinand and the "Sunshine Boys."

"He did loaf a little in the last little bit—only the ones behind him couldn't catch up," Whittingham said.

Under left-handed whipping near the end, Ferdinand crossed the finish line 2¼ lengths in front of English invader Bold Arrangement.

The key word after this Derby was "emotion." "I had a few tears in my eyes coming back to the winner's circle," Shoemaker said. "To tell you the truth, I thought, 'Well, old Jack Nicklaus did it, and I did it, too.' It was certainly very emotional."

"I never felt more emotional after a race," Whittingham declared.

Assessing his four Derby victories, Shoemaker said, "This was the best one of the whole group. I'm in the twilight of my career, and I might not get another chance to win it again."

Whittingham was another reason why Ferdinand's victory "was the best Derby of the four," Shoemaker added. "To do it for a guy like Charlie, who I think is the best trainer and the best horseman in the business. He takes his time; he lets his horses tell him when they're ready. He didn't rush this horse or put blinkers on him, something somebody else might do."

The 1986 Derby drew some outstanding runners, including three who would win Eclipse Awards—Ferdinand, 1987 Horse of the Year; Snow Chief, champion three-year-old colt of 1986; and Groovy, best sprinter of 1987. In addition, third-place Derby finisher Broad Brush earned $2,656,793 in his three-year career. Broad Brush, incidentally, was sired by Ack Ack, the 1971 Horse of the Year trained by Whittingham.

As much as Ferdinand is remembered for his Derby victory, the colt's four-year-old campaign produced that Horse of the Year title following a thrilling nose victory over 1987 Kentucky Derby winner Alysheba in the Breeders' Cup Classic. With Shoemaker timing his move perfectly,

Ferdinand overtook Judge Angelucci and then held off the late charge by Alysheba to win the 1¼-mile race at Hollywood Park. "I didn't want to make the lead too soon," Shoemaker said, "but I was kind of worried at about the sixteenth pole whether I was going to get by the Judge or not. I saw Alysheba coming up on the outside, and I just waited, waited, waited, then I shook my stick at him and let him go to the lead. He saw Alysheba coming in just enough time to put in a little extra effort, and he got the job done."

In the 1988 Derby, Shoemaker and Whittingham joined up again for another shot at the roses, but Lively One could do no better than twelfth. That Derby was a record twenty-sixth—and last—appearance for Shoemaker in the race as a jockey. In 1989, the seventy-six-year-old Whittingham won his second Derby, this time with Sunday Silence, who earned the Horse of the Year title that season.

Shoemaker, who retired in 1990 as the world's winningest rider, with 8,833 victories, turned to training. After being paralyzed from the neck down in a one-car accident in 1991, he returned to the Derby in 1993 with Diazo, who finished fifth. That was the year that Bull Inthe Heather, a son of Ferdinand, finished eleventh as the second choice in the Derby.

Ferdinand, who began his stud career at Claiborne Farm, was sold to Japanese interests in 1994 and sent to the Orient.

Howard Keck announced his retirement from racing in 1995 and dispersed his blue-blooded racing and breeding stock in 1996.

As for Charlie Whittingham, he's still getting up early each morning, heading to the racetrack and doing what he does best—train horses.

Whittingham, who turned eighty-three on April 13, 1996, started Corker in the Derby that spring. Corker didn't win, but Whittingham's appearance on the scene was proof that a man never gets too old to dream about the Kentucky Derby.

Genuine Risk, ridden by Jacinto Vasquez, captured the 1980 Kentucky Derby by a length. (Photo courtesy Churchill Downs Incorporated/Kinetic Corporation)

5

As Genuine as They Come

"THEY'RE IN THE FINAL FURLONG, it's Genuine Risk, and she's genuine! Here comes Rumbo on the outside! Genuine Risk is going to win it! Genuine Risk by one!"

In announcing the 1980 Kentucky Derby, Dave Johnson couldn't have come up with a better line in those final yards. "It's Genuine Risk, and she's genuine!" As genuine as they come, you might add.

Genuine Risk came in 1980 to win the Derby and then run second in both the Preakness and Belmont. She was only the second filly to win the Derby and the first to start in all three legs of the Triple Crown. Since then, Winning Colors has become the third filly to capture the Derby, doing so in 1988, and the second to compete in the other two legs as well, though she didn't fare as well in those two races, running third in the Preakness and last in the Belmont.

Genuine Risk was voted champion three-year-old filly of 1980 and was enshrined in racing's Hall of Fame in 1986, her first year of eligibility. She was a popular racehorse, a gallant runner, and her story is one that will be told for years to come. It involves not only her racing days but her days in retirement as well. Suffering one misfortune after another, Genuine Risk was unable to produce a live foal until she was sixteen.

Breeding, like racing, is not a place for the fainthearted,

51

and Bert Firestone, the filly's owner with his wife, Diana, never gave up hope that the famous horse would have a foal. "Hopefully, we'll get a foal out of her," he said in 1990. "You never can tell. You just have to keep trying, that's all. We feel that she was a great filly. I'd love to have another one like her."

The Firestones have always had faith in Genuine Risk. If they hadn't believed in her, she never would have been in Louisville on the first Saturday in May of her three-year-old season.

A $32,000 yearling acquisition, the daughter of Exclusive Native and Virtuous won the first six races of her career, all against fillies, before trying the boys for the first time in the 1980 Wood Memorial. She ran a good third in that race, beaten only by a length and a half, but afterward her trainer, LeRoy Jolley, said she wouldn't go to the Kentucky Derby. However, the Firestones decided she deserved a chance to run for the roses, and she was sent to Louisville, the first filly to start in the Derby since Silver Spoon in 1959.

Listed at 10-1 odds in the program's morning line, Genuine Risk was sent off at 13.30-1. The starting lineup of thirteen included favored Rockhill Native, the champion two-year-old male of 1979, and Plugged Nickle, the second choice who would go on to win the 1980 Eclipse Award as best sprinter. Also in the field were the stretch-running Rumbo, the consistent Jaklin Klugman, and Super Moment.

When Regret (1915) and Winning Colors won the Derby, the other two fillies to do so, they led all the way, but Genuine Risk came from off the pace. Ridden flawlessly by Jacinto Vasquez, she was seventh in the early going and moved up going down the backstretch.

Genuine Risk made an impressive move rounding the far turn, overtaking four or five opponents on the outside and advancing to the lead near the five-sixteenths pole. Vasquez hit her once right-handed in the upper stretch and six times left-handed the rest of the way as she ran the final quarter-mile in 24²/₅ seconds. Rumbo was flying at the finish, covering the last quarter in a scorching :23²/₅.

Genuine Risk's final quarter was faster than the previous three Derby winners, each of whom wound up in the Hall of Fame also. Seattle Slew, the 1977 Derby winner, ran his final quarter in :26¹/₅, Affirmed (1978) in :25²/₅, and Spectacular Bid (1979) in :24⁴/₅.

A fast final quarter didn't come as a surprise to Mrs. Firestone. "I didn't have any hesitation about entering her at all," she said after the Derby. "I knew she could do it. Something inside me always knew that she had the potential to beat the colts. I just knew I had to give her the chance. The Derby is a very testing race, but I felt it suited her way of running and her breeding. She's bred to get a fast final quarter. She had shown that in the past, and she showed it again today."

Jim McKay, the ABC sports commentator, had asked Jolley after the Wood whether it created a problem for him in regard to running Genuine Risk in the Derby. "It's no problem for me," Jolley told McKay. "We're not going." So after the Derby, McKay reminded Jolley on the presentation stand that he hadn't wanted to run the filly in the Derby. Jolley smiled and replied, "Well, Jim, you have to keep an open mind about these things."

Winning the Derby gave Genuine Risk a special place in turf history, and later Firestone commented on the importance of that race. "Whatever Genuine Risk does now, she has already won the greatest race in the world," he said. "Friends call up and people write letters, and people you don't know come up to congratulate you—and they don't know races. It is the greatest race."

Genuine Risk's second-place finish in the Preakness was controversial. It will always be debated as to whether Angel Cordero, Jr., aboard the victorious Codex, actually interfered with Genuine Risk turning for home. But what isn't open to dispute is the way the Maryland stewards fumbled the ball immediately after the race, failing even to post the inquiry sign, leaving it to Vasquez to have to claim a foul.

The Firestone filly went on to run second to long-shot Temperence Hill in the Belmont Stakes, losing by two lengths after leading at the stretch call.

Genuine Risk finished in the money in all fifteen of her starts, completing her career with ten victories, three seconds, and two thirds to her credit. Following her retirement, Genuine Risk was sent to the court of Secretariat himself, the first mating ever between two Derby winners. The breeding session took place at Claiborne Farm. "You know, it was a great moment in racing history," Claiborne manager John Sosby said at the time. "It's something you add to the list of things that you've seen and will never forget. You was there when it happened."

Said Dr. Walter Kaufman, the Claiborne vet, "She was just a doll. She was as docile as could be. And he's a magnificent animal."

Hopes were high for Genuine Risk, and all the racing world awaited the arrival of this foal. However, the following spring sad news came from Waterford, Virginia. On April 4, 1983, Genuine Risk had delivered a stillborn chestnut colt at the Firestones' Catoctin Stud. John Moore, broodmare manager at Catoctin, was quoted as saying, "She knew the foal was dead. She got up fine. She'd look at the foal and then go away. Then she would come back and look at it again and go away. A mare will nicker for the foal to get up. She did that. Then what they do is begin to cover it up. They will shove the straw over it to cover it up. She did that. She knows. Then I took the foal."

Genuine Risk was "two weeks overdue, which is a common occurrence in horses, and this tragedy was completely unexpected," said a statement issued by the farm. "Mr. and Mrs. Firestone have announced that they will now breed Genuine Risk back to Secretariat this year. Previously, they had planned to send her to Nijinsky II, which they now hope to do in 1984."

In 1990, Dr. Richard Holder (of Hagyard-Davidson-McGee Associates) recalled the examination after she returned to Kentucky: "She had a very difficult foaling. The fetus died, and there was extensive injury to the internal lining of her reproductive tract—the inside of the uterus, cervix, and vagina. So essentially, I think after that dystocia [difficult birth], the problems that she had were probably due to the fact that she needed time to repair from the damage done."

When Genuine Risk was bred back to Secretariat in 1983, she didn't conceive. The next year she was bred to 1977 Epsom Derby winner The Minstrel, and again she was barren. Then in 1985, she was sent to Ireland to be bred to Cure the Blues at the Firestones' Gilltown Stud.

"A change in atmosphere might help sometimes," Firestone later said. "We had our own farm there and our own vet. But the same thing happened over there, so we sent her back to America."

After being barren to Cure the Blues in Ireland, Genuine Risk did become pregnant each of the next three years, but she lost the fetus each time "within the first trimester, which is under ninety days," according to Holder. In the first two years, 1986 and 1987, she was bred to Dixieland Band, and in 1988 she was bred back to Cure the Blues, who was standing at Pillar Stud in Kentucky by that time.

In 1989, she was bred back to Cure the Blues on April 19, and she carried the foal 259 days before losing it on January 3, 1990, at the Firestones' Big Sink Farm, near Versailles, Kentucky. Except for the stillborn colt that she had in 1983, this was the longest she had ever carried a foal up until that time. "It really wasn't any fault of hers," Firestone said. "It was just an unfortunate thing. Everyone was really disappointed when that happened. But from what the vets say, there's no reason she won't get in foal again this next time. And maybe we won't have any bad luck with her next time. The only thing we can do is keep trying."

Holder elaborated on Genuine Risk's abortion, saying

that the necropsy report from the University of Kentucky noted that the only thing that could be found wrong with the foal was a twisted umbilical cord. "That is really just bad luck and not really a knock against the mare," Holder said.

Genuine Risk had suffered more than her share of bad luck in retirement, but in 1990 Holder sounded an optimistic note for the future. "The first two or three years that I had her after she got back from Ireland, when you looked at her on speculum exam, she really did not look that good. There was a lot of streaking and apparent inflammation in the cervix. She had a look that kinda bothered you.

"However, last year when we examined her, it was like looking at a normal cervix. We were optimistic last year. This year when I looked at her, she looked as good as she did last year, maybe even a little better. This year after the abortion, she looks great. She cultures clean; she's doing everything just right. Hopefully, without any bad luck, we'll have a normal-term fetus. The mare certainly looks better reproductively than she's ever looked.

"I think essentially what's happened is she needed several years to recover from the dystocia that she had and then she was a little bit of a chronically infected mare. I think that's what happened with these ones that aborted in the first trimester. After she became pregnant, the placenta and the membranes had some kind of bacteria that was seeded in there that reestablished itself and killed the fetus, and she aborted it. We're certainly hoping that her problems are behind her and she'll go on and be completely normal from here on."

Some people in racing believe that great racemares don't make outstanding broodmares, but Holder said, "I think for every great racemare that didn't make it reproductively, there's certainly been an equal number that *did*. Look at Relaxing, who was a champion mare and the dam of Easy Goer, and Fanfreluche [dam of L'Enjoleur and D'Accord].

"I've heard that if people had a choice between a great racemare or her full sister that wasn't such a great racemare, they'd take the full sister. I don't really go along with that.

"Everybody really wants her to have a baby," Holder added. "It's kinda neat to see the public sentiment and involvement and interest in her pregnancy, because I've never had another mare that people asked me all year long, 'How's she doing?' Certainly everybody's behind her, and I'm encouraged, really. We seem to be getting closer and closer."

Finally, in 1993, Genuine Risk carried a foal, by Rahy, all the way. Boarded at Mr. and Mrs. Robert N. Clay's Three Chimneys Farm near Midway, Kentucky, she was the focus of much attention in the days leading up to her successful delivery. She was due to foal on April 20 . . . and the countdown was on. In mid-April, Three Chimneys general manager Dan Rosenberg said, "We're in a holding pattern right now. We're just watching and waiting along with the rest of the world."

The foal—a colt—arrived on May 15. Generating international interest, his birth at Rood and Riddle Equine Hospital near Lexington was announced on national television. Genuine Risk—or "Jenny," as she is called around the farm—could have used a private secretary to handle all of the mail and hundreds of calls that came her way. Some of the mail was addressed to *The New Mommy* or *Ms. Genuine Risk.* Roses, congratulatory bouquets, photographs, letters, cards, drawings, poems, stories, and carrots (real and stuffed) were sent in honor of Genuine Risk's first foal. Three Chimneys received congratulatory faxes from Europe and Japan.

Appropriately enough, Genuine Risk's first foal was named Genuine Reward. Unfortunately, he never made it to the races. He developed a severe case of bucked shins and suffered a series of colds and other misfortunes.

In 1996, Genuine Risk produced her second foal, a colt sired by Chief Honcho. This colt carries the blood of a genuine champion. His mother proved that she was genuine on Derby Day 1980.

King Ranch owner Robert Kleberg, Jr., with Assault. (Photo courtesy King Ranch Archives, King Ranch, Inc.)

6

Assault: The Little Horse with the Heart of a Giant

IN 1946, A LITTLE HORSE came along from the mighty state of Texas to sweep the Triple Crown of Thoroughbred racing. Assault was his name, and racing was his game.

Not only was Assault a native of Texas, but so were his owner, Robert J. Kleberg, Jr., and trainer, Max Hirsch.

The story of Assault is one that epitomizes the heart of a racehorse. From the moment that he stepped on a sharp object as a youngster at King Ranch, Assault was plagued by physical problems throughout his career, but he had the heart of a giant. He was "a champion of champions," King Ranch veterinarian Dr. J. K. Northway asserted. "He was always crippled, and a horse with less determination would have quit." During his career, he had to deal with that foot problem and overcome several splints, a troublesome knee, a wrenched ankle, and bleeding.

Assault, foaled at the great King Ranch of Robert Kleberg, Jr., was sired by 1936 Kentucky Derby winner Bold Venture and was out of Igual, who was so unhealthy as a foal that a decision was almost made to destroy her. Fortunately, Igual's problem was discovered—an abscess under a stifle— and was cleared up with treatment. Even so, her early difficulties slowed her development and precluded her ever being put into training.

Assault was her third foal, and he likewise encountered trouble at an early age, stepping on a sharp object (take your pick: a nail, surveyor's stake, pointed stick, or maybe just a thorn) that pierced his right front foot. In trying to protect the hoof while it healed, Assault developed an unorthodox gait, and when he was sent to Hirsch, he didn't make a favorable first impression.

In early April of Assault's three-year-old season, Hirsch said, "When he came up from Texas, I didn't think he'd train at all. But he's never shown any sign that it hurts him. When he walks or trots you'd think he was going to fall down. I think that while the foot still hurt him he got in the habit of protecting it with an awkward gait, and now he keeps it up. But he gallops true. There isn't a thing wrong with his action when he goes fast."

Assault's right forefoot never fully grew and was weak. The wall of his hoof was thin in front, making it difficult to find sufficient room to anchor a nail. He required careful attention from the blacksmith throughout his career.

In 1946, the King Ranch silks—brown, white running *W* front and back, brown bars on white sleeves, and brown-and-white cap—were making their second appearance in the Derby. King Ranch's Dispose had finished sixth in the 1941 Derby.

Assault was the eleventh of Hirsch's fourteen Derby starters. Hirsch started his first Derby horse in 1915—Norse King, who finished next to last. Hirsch won the 1936 Run for the Roses with Bold Venture, who would sire another Derby winner (1950) for the trainer and King Ranch—Texas-bred Middleground.

Hirsch, born July 30, 1880 in Fredericksburg, Texas, re-membered unfriendly Indians in the nearby hills as a youngster. Bitten by the racing bug as a boy, he rode horses at wildcat county-fair meetings in Texas when he was just ten and ran away from home at the age of twelve or thirteen to become a jockey. He was an exercise rider for a year before donning silks as a full-fledged jockey. At nineteen, he became too heavy to continue his career as a rider, and the next year he took out his first trainer's license. He went on to become a Hall of Fame trainer who was based in New York during the racing season.

Assault was named by Kleberg's wife. He explained years later:

> Of course, Assault being by Bold Venture, one could guess that the name Assault is appropriate. There is the additional thing that Bold Venture's grandsire, Ultimus, was by Commando. This, too, could have entered into the selection of the name.

Kleberg, born on March 29, 1896 in Corpus Christi, became associated with his father in the King Ranch operation in 1916. Following his father's death in 1932, Kleberg took over as president of the King Ranch Corporation. Subsequent to the King Ranch master's death in 1974 at the age of seventy-eight, *The Thoroughbred Record* magazine wrote:

> King Ranch's thoroughbred breeding program scarcely could be classified as conventional, but it was by no means fully illustrative of Mr. Kleberg's daring departures from standard routes. He did practice "line breeding," and inbreeding to an extent that others perhaps would not choose to venture, and he did employ as breeding stock some horses that other breeders looked at askance if they looked at them at all. Yet, these experiments were mild compared to the King Ranch procedures in the breeding of cattle, the corporation's main purpose, and the concomitant breeding of ranch horses to work the cattle. (While not an original purpose of the corporation, the production of oil on its vast lands was a beneficial sideline which presumably helped finance expansion of the cattle empire.)

Following Assault's success in the Derby, Kleberg told newsmen, "This comes of line breeding to Domino." Kleberg believed that Assault greatly resembled his maternal grandsire, Equipoise, a horse whom the King Ranch owner had long admired.

J. A. Estes wrote after the '46 Derby:

> As a creator of new breeds and new types of live-stock, Mr. Kleberg has learned to work skillfully with inbreeding and selection on the basis of type and performance, and he carries his methods over into his Thoroughbred breeding ventures. Probably as well as any breeder of race horses in America, he knows the types he wants and the strains most likely to produce them. He works in the medium of heredity with the steady hand and eye of a man at a lathe turning out a part for a machine. When he misses (as all breeders do, far more frequently than they succeed), he tosses aside the failure and starts over with the same technique.

Igual produced thirteen foals altogether, and ten of them were sired by Bold Venture, with Assault being the first. Two others of those ten also were stakes winners—Postillion (a colt foaled in 1950) and On Your Own (a 1951 filly). Assault was the only champion to come from the Bold Venture-Igual breeding formula, but one was good enough. He was the best horse ever bred by Kleberg.

Assault was referred to as *The Club-Footed Comet*, which made for good reading but wasn't accurate. At least the part about the clubfoot wasn't correct. His right front foot "was just dished a little and a trifle rough in front," one writer noted.

But there's no mistaking that on certain days he was a comet. One of those afternoons came on the first Saturday in May in 1946, when he streaked to an eight-length victory in the Kentucky Derby. "After the first quarter, I knew he was full of run and wanted to run," his jockey, Warren Mehrtens, said afterward. "We were fourth, then third down the backside, slipped through along the rail to take the lead, and then to keep his mind on his work, I slashed him several times."

Assault, an 8-1 shot in the Derby, had never been favored in any of his previous twelve starts. In his lone stakes victory at age two, the 5½-furlong Flash, he triumphed at 70-1. His average price was 23-1 in his dozen races leading up to the Derby.

On Derby Day in 1946 Assault was much the best in a field of seventeen. Tommy Fitzgerald wrote in *The Courier-Journal:*

> It wasn't Assault in the Kentucky Derby yesterday. It was murder!
>
> The way he ran away with the race in the stretch you'd have thought Assault was being chased by 16 cops.
>
> The Lone Star yesterday from the Lone Star State won by the width of Texas. As he flew away from them in the stretch, the only hope the other horses seemed to have of ever catching Assault was to hang around when the race was over and wait for him to revisit the scene of his crime.

Afterward, Kleberg said he was proudest of the fact that Assault "was bred in Texas and out of a Texas broodmare." He said he "always wanted to see a Texas-bred hoss win the Derby, and I'm glad we did it."

The 1946 Derby result sent vibrations all the way to Kingsville. The Associated Press reported:

> Kingsville, this little city at the edge of vast King Ranch, thrilled today to the victory by Assault in the Kentucky Derby. King Ranch, a mighty domain of almost 1,000,000 acres, is birthplace of Assault.
>
> Not only is Assault the first Texas horse to win the greatest race of them all but he is the first horse sired on King Ranch to be sent to the Derby by Robert Kleberg, Jr., manager of the vast property.
>
> Kleberg, brother of Richard Kleberg, former congressman from Texas, tried for the Roses once before but it was with Dispose, Kentucky-born. That was the year of Whirlaway.

In Kingsville the folks just nod and tell you they
knew it all the time—that King Ranch was bound to
sire a champion.

Assault was finally favored in his fourteenth start, going
off at 7-5 in the Preakness. After escaping trouble in the
early going (he was bothered by Natchez), he moved out to
a four-length lead at the stretch call. At the wire, though, he
was in front by just a neck over Lord Boswell. Warren
Mehrtens, who rode Assault, blamed himself for the close
call in the Preakness, recalling, "I moved too soon, and
when I hit him once at the head of the stretch, he ducked
with me down to the rail. I was afraid that if I hit him anymore, he might sulk and back up, so I didn't hit him again.
Maybe I hit him in the wrong place or he didn't expect it or
something, but he ducked from it. I think he'd have won by
further if I had hit him."

Assault "got slammed around all through the first
eighth," Hirsch said when analyzing the Preakness. "The
jockey had to make a lot of use of him to regain the lost
ground, and maybe he got a little flustered and made too
much use of him. Anyway, Assault had to run the whole race
without drawing a deep breath. Sure he got tired in the
stretch. Who wouldn't?"

In the Belmont Stakes, the betting public made Lord
Boswell a slight favorite over Assault, but the King Ranch
colt won by three lengths to become racing's seventh Triple
Crown champion. "The only time I was worried was coming
out of the gate, when Assault stumbled," jockey Warren
Mehrtens said afterward. "He recovered at once, and we
were never in difficulty again. I had more confidence this
time than in either the Derby or Preakness, but I still can't
believe we've won the Triple Crown."

Accepting the trophy, Kleberg said, "We're deeply happy,
and we feel others will agree with us now that Assault is a
great horse. I want particularly to compliment Max Hirsch
on a great training job."

All three Triple Crown races increased their purses to the $100,000-added level in 1946, helping Assault to earn a record $424,195 in his Horse of the Year campaign. The former one-season mark—$308,275—was set by Gallant Fox in 1930.

In 1947, Assault won five straight handicaps under high weights: the Grey Lag (128), Dixie (129), Suburban (130), Brooklyn (133), and Butler (135). Stymie was a victim in four of those races, Gallorette in one. The Butler, the colt's seventh straight victory stretching back to his final two starts of 1946, was the greatest race of Assault's career. Seemingly beaten well inside the eighth pole, he shot forward under Eddie Arcaro's determined handling and charged between Gallorette (117) and Stymie (126) to win by a head over the latter.

The courageous Assault overcame interference more than once in the race, and afterward Arcaro said, "He ran a big race. I was bothered when Stymie made his move. [Bobby] Permane's whip hit Assault in the head three or four times."

In *The Blood-Horse* magazine, Joe H. Palmer wrote, "My own opinion of Assault was high going into the race, but it is considerably higher now than if he had simply run down his field with clear sailing. It gave him a chance to show more heart than he has ever shown before and we wouldn't have known quite how great a horse Assault is if he hadn't been forced to do it the hard way."

Assault twice was the world's top money winner during his 1947 winning streak, holding the lead for two weeks after the Brooklyn ($576,670) and for one week following the Butler ($613,370).

On September 27, 1947, Assault lost to Armed by six or eight lengths in a Belmont Park match race that should never have taken place. With Assault suffering from a splint problem, no betting was allowed, which was a wise decision.

Following a fifth-place finish in the 1948 Widener

Assault in 1947. (Photo courtesy King Ranch Archives, King Ranch, Inc.)

Exercise rider Jose Angel ("Pie") Garcia aboard Assault in 1948. (Photo courtesy King Ranch Archives, King Ranch, Inc.)

Handicap, Assault was retired to stand in Kentucky, but he appeared to be sterile. He was sent to Texas and sired three foals from quarter-horse mares while turned out.

Assault was brought back to the races in 1949. *The New York Times* reported on June 24:

> Assault hasn't flown silks since the Widener Handicap in February of 1948. He ran fifth in it and injured his left foreleg so severely that it looked as if he had reached the end of his racing trail. He was tried at stud, but failed to make a success of it.
>
> Now, after a winter of training in Texas and a tune-up period at Belmont Park, he's ready for the racing wars again at the age of 6. He has filled out; in trials he has shown much of his old lick.

Assault lost the first race in his comeback by a nose and then won the 1¼-mile Brooklyn Handicap, his final stakes success. The following year he scored the eighteenth—and final—victory of his career, capturing an overnight race at Hollywood Park. After finishing seventh in the Hollywood Gold Cup, he was permanently retired with earnings of $675,470.

Assault spent the last twenty-one years of his life at King Ranch in Texas. The phenomenon of his having gotten several quarter-horse mares in foal was an interesting one. Instead of risking any more Thoroughbred mares on Assault, King Ranch veterinarian Dr. J. K. Northway "turned him out in pasture with, oh, eight or ten quarter-horse mares because we've got plenty of them around," John Cypher, assistant to the King Ranch president at the time, said in a 1977 interview about the ranch's veterinarians. "This sometimes happens that a horse won't breed in confinement or won't hand mate but will breed in pasture. We've even seen that in other Thoroughbred stallions. We had a gelding around here for some time that was a son of his, and we had a mare in our quarter-horse band that was a daughter. The horses were never used in any way except here on the ranch. We don't know why he would get just a couple of mares in foal and then never show anything again. Just one of those things that we can't explain."

Cypher said Assault showed an interest in breeding to Thoroughbred mares. "Oh, there wasn't anything wrong with him mechanically," he said. "He bred just as well as any other horse. It's just that his semen was inactive."

In a story appearing in the August 13, 1971 issue of *The Louisville Times*, Northway was quoted as saying that Assault, who was twenty-eight years old, was "happy in his retirement and doing just fine for someone his age." Northway continued, "He couldn't be better. He has his own 10-acre green pasture, and he enjoys the freedom."

Less than three weeks later, Assault was put down on September 1, a quarter of a century after he won the Triple Crown. The day before, he had broken a bone in his left leg, near the shoulder. "I never trained a better horse," Hirsch said. "Man o' War had everything, but so did Assault."

Years later, Mehrtens, who rode Assault to victory in all three Triple Crown races, looked back on this champion and said, "He was a lovable horse, and he had the heart of a giant."

Assault was buried at King Ranch "under a simple marble stone in a neat row of graves that includes Middleground's," *The Courier-Journal*'s Jennie Rees wrote in 1996. "Assault is said to have been buried in a running stance, facing west, in cavalry tradition."

On Derby Day in 1996, King Ranch hosted in Texas a commemorative gala in honor of Assault's fiftieth anniversary sweep of the Triple Crown. "This event provides a wonderful opportunity to look back and commemorate not only a great champion, but the role that King Ranch and Robert J. Kleberg, Jr., played in creating a viable Thoroughbred industry in Texas," said Jack Hunt, president and chief executive officer of King Ranch.

Assault (1943-71) was a little horse who stood tall among racing's giants.

7

Diary of a Champion, Skip Away

When trainer Hubert ("Sonny") Hine brought Skip Away to Kentucky in the spring of 1996, it was my privilege to follow the colt's progress during his time at Keeneland Race Course and Churchill Downs. Checking each day for a month with Sonny was quite a learning experience for me—not only about horses but about life. He and his wife, Carolyn, in whose name Skip Away raced, could write a book about how to enjoy horses and life at the same time.

In more than thirty years of covering the Kentucky Derby, I've never been closer to a trainer and owner than I was to Sonny and Carolyn in the month leading up to the Derby. If I don't enjoy another such experience the rest of my life, at least I will always have the memory of this lovely couple who came to Kentucky, enjoyed Southern hospitality, and made such a favorable impression on the people they met.

April 5—Hine, a veteran trainer, knows his way around the racetrack, but he didn't know his way to Keeneland Race Course this morning. He had never previously been to the Lexington track. "I was so confused," he said. "I didn't know where I was at. You'd have thought Lexington was New York City, I was so confused. And being a man who doesn't like to ask directions, I was in trouble. I just got in some wrong streets."

Hine then decided to follow two cars. "I said, 'Anybody

69

up at five o'clock in the morning must be going to the race-track.' The next thing I knew, I thought I was in a park." Instead, he was at picturesque Keeneland.

Sonny has an interesting background. Upon graduation from high school in 1948, he hitchhiked to Charles Town racetrack, and he's been on and off the track since then. He saddled his first winner, Miss Economy, in 1948 at Marlboro Race Course.

He was employed for almost two years as a fingerprint specialist by the Federal Bureau of Investigation. He left the FBI in 1950, then four years later went to work as a State Department investigator. He was assigned duty in Hong Kong. "They needed somebody with an investigative back-ground who could speak Chinese," says Sonny, who can speak the Mandarin dialect of the Chinese language.

Since 1957, Sonny has been training full time, and now in the spring of 1996 the sixty-five-year-old horseman was at Keeneland Race Course preparing Florida-bred Kentucky Derby candidate Skip Away for the $700,000 Toyota Blue Grass Stakes on April 13. Skip Away was bred by Anna Marie Barnhart. Sonny, who has a sharp eye for horses, purchased the gray/roan colt for $22,500 at the Ocala Breeders' Sales Company's 1995 Calder Two-Year-Old Select Sale.

"I liked the way he went," Sonny would recall in the days leading up to the Derby. "It turned out he was a Skip Trial, which made it better. I trained the father."

Actually, when Skip Away left the auction ring, he had been sold for $30,000. When the colt was vetted, a chip was discovered in an ankle. An arbitration board ruled that the chip was sufficient grounds to return the purchase and Sonny gave Skip Away back, but he changed his mind when he was driving home. He found the consignor, and they agreed to sell the colt for $22,500. The consignor suggested that Hine take the difference—$7,500—and have the chip removed. But the chip has never been a problem, and Hine, who can't even tell you which ankle it's in, didn't have it re-moved.

Sonny recalled that he offered one of his clients, Robert Ades, an interest in Skip Away. "I was going to sell him a half or third—whatever he wanted. He said, 'No, I don't want a damaged horse.'"

Sonny's brother-in-law, Dr. Irving Seaman, also turned down a chance to own an interest in Skip Away. "He said, 'I'm like Bob. I don't want part of him.'"

Sonny and Carolyn have received offers for Skip Away, but they say he's not for sale. "This is ours to enjoy," Sonny said. "In thirty-four years, we've never taken three consecutive days off."

Trained to the Minute for the Blue Grass

It was my observation that Sonny came to Lexington for one specific purpose—to train his colt to *win* the Toyota Blue Grass. Where other trainers might view the Blue Grass merely as a tune-up for the Kentucky Derby, Sonny prepared Skip Away for this race. He wasn't interested in finishing fourth or fifth and finding some weak excuse that would allow him to send the colt on to Louisville. As he put it on April 5, his first day at Keeneland, "If I don't run big in the Blue Grass, I won't run in the Derby."

The Blue Grass purse was elevated from $500,000 to $700,000 for the 1996 running, so the prize money certainly was appealing enough. Skip Away came into the Blue Grass off a third-place finish in the Florida Derby, a race in which he didn't have quite the best of trips. Moreover, he wasn't as tight as he should have been for the Florida Derby. Sonny would have him just right for the Blue Grass.

As far as the Derby was concerned, Sonny wasn't interested in running for the roses unless his colt belonged in the race. Too bad more people don't approach the Derby with that kind of an attitude.

April 8—Skip Away turned in a blazing five-furlong workout in 58²/₅ seconds under jockey Shane Sellers. Stablemate

Maketherightmove, a five-year-old horse, broke off about a sixteenth of a mile ahead of Skip Away. Skip Away caught Maketherightmove near the finish line and passed him in an eye-catching move. His time was the morning's fastest for the twenty-three workouts at five furlongs.

"He went fairly easy," Sellers said. "I just let him finish up. It was an unbelievable work. It was very impressive, believe me. I'm very excited about him."

"I wanted something good in him," Sonny said. "He hasn't run in quite a while. I was pleased with the work. I imagine he'll be bouncing and playing around the shedrow [barn] tomorrow."

April 9—Sonny said Skip Away came out of his workout in good order. "At feed time [the previous night], he was raising heck," the trainer said. "It didn't take anything out of him. He's sharp. Just need a little luck. Good trip, that's all we need."

April 10—The daily report on Skip Away couldn't be better. "My horse is coming in great—in great shape," Sonny said. "He's fit—getting good."

April 11—"This horse is in such great shape," Sonny said.
The veteran trainer had "a gut feeling" about the Blue Grass. "I'm very relaxed. Just need some luck."

April 12—Sonny continued to exude confidence in Skip Away. "Everything's fine," he said. "He's in great shape for this race. I'm not coming up empty."

April 13—On the morning of the Blue Grass, Sonny was walking through the Keeneland stable area. The highlight race of Keeneland's spring meeting was just hours away. "He's ready," Sonny said. "He's got the conditioning now. I feel good about him."

What did Skip Away have to do in the Blue Grass to earn a trip to the Kentucky Derby? "Hope he runs his race—runs his race and has a good trip—and he'll certainly be on the road [to Louisville]," Sonny replied. "Time will tell. Got to get by today first. Today's race is so important to us."

A luncheon was held in the Keeneland Room for the track's board of directors, Kentucky governor Paul Patton and his wife, and many of the owners and trainers of Blue Grass horses. Carolyn told Governor Patton that Skip Away was training well, and that's all he needed to hear. He bet on a winner.

Skip Away, a big, powerful runner, captured the 1⅛-mile Blue Grass by at least six lengths and was timed in 1:47⅕ on a wet-fast track, breaking the great Round Table's stakes record of 1:47⅖ set in 1957. "I told everybody around me I wouldn't be surprised if he won by eight," Sonny said afterward. "We came here because we knew the Blue Grass

Skip Away, piloted by Shane Sellers, set a stakes record in winning the 1996 Toyota Blue Grass Stakes at Keeneland Race Course. (Photo courtesy Keeneland Association by Bill Straus)

Skip Away, with Shane Sellers up, in the winner's circle following his triumph in the 1996 Toyota Blue Grass Stakes at Keeneland Race Course. (Photo courtesy Keeneland Association by Bill Straus)

Trainer Hubert ("Sonny") Hine (third from left), owner Carolyn Hine (fourth from left), jockey Shane Sellers, and Kentucky governor Paul Patton (second from right) took part in the presentation ceremony following Skip Away's victory in the 1996 Toyota Blue Grass Stakes at Keeneland Race Course. (Photo courtesy Keeneland Association by Bill Straus)

would be the most competitive race. We did not want to deceive ourselves."

A Marriage Made in Heaven

Sonny and Carolyn met on a blind date in Florida and were married on October 14, 1962. "Everybody should be as lucky as we've been," Sonny said. "We've sure had a great relationship."

"We're not only husband and wife," Carolyn said. "We're good friends. We love being with each other. We enjoy each other's company. He's my best friend. I'm his best friend. We do everything together. I'm very much involved in the business."

She told John Crittenden of *The Palm Beach Post,* "I have no children, and I don't belong to a country club. And I still have no time. The horses keep you busy."

After the Blue Grass, Sonny told the media, "I dedicated this race to my wife. I can't be happier for her."

April 16—In hindsight, Skip Away figured to run a big race in the Blue Grass. He had trained superbly for the race, coming into it off two beneficial workouts—the :58²⁄₅ drill following a 1:11³⁄₅ six-furlong move on March 30 at Gulfstream Park. Those two workouts, both bullet moves, set him up perfectly for the Blue Grass. His previous workouts this season had been too easy for this talented colt. "They looked like fast works, but he wasn't doing anything," Sonny said.

April 18—Skip Away was measured by Cecil Seaman, Thoroughbred analyst from Lexington. "He was ecstatic about the horse's measurements," Sonny said.

Skip Away's Dosage Index number was higher than 4, meaning that people who believe in this foolish theory would discount the colt's chances in the Derby. "I'd rather have a runner than a Dosage," said Sonny, who knew he had a runner in Skip Away.

Seaman later would say of Skip Away, "He evaluates to make a lot of lifetime starts. He should be a very sound horse. He's capable of running the Belmont distance of a mile and a half without any trouble biomechanically, and I would forget about the Dosage on him because he's got the leverage and the point of gravity to run over a mile and a half. He evaluates into the top one-half of 1 percent of all horses."

Sonny related that trainer Tom Skiffington "said I'm living his dream—running your own horses in the Derby."

Standing near the Keeneland paddock before the last race, Carolyn talked about all the wonderful people she and Sonny have met in racing and about her love for the sport. Looking ahead to the Derby, she said wistfully, "I just hope we get lucky. After thirty-some years, it's time."

April 20—Skip Away was vanned to Churchill Downs today. In a precautionary measure, Sonny sent two other horses—one to be stabled on each side of Skip Away. It seems that in 1992 when Sonny ran Technology in the Derby, the colt came down with a light cough the day before the Derby. He said the horse stabled next to Technology was sick. "Technology's temperature stayed normal," Sonny said. "His appetite was good. We took a quick blood study, and his white count was normal. But he was never the same horse after the Derby. He was susceptible to any virus that came along. I'm just trying not to make the same mistakes twice." Technology finished tenth as the Derby's second choice.

Contemplating Skip Away's training schedule for the Derby, Sonny said, "You certainly don't want to overdo it. You don't want to underdo it. It's a fine line."

April 22—Sonny appeared at Keeneland at 5:15 A.M. to

look after his horses there and then he headed to Churchill Downs, arriving with Carolyn at 7:20 A.M. or so. With horses in two locations, Sonny and Carolyn had rooms in both the Campbell House in Lexington and the Executive Inn in Louisville for the time being.

Pete Johnson, trusted Hine assistant trainer since 1979, was sitting in a chair in front of Skip Away's stall, holding the colt's shank. Skip Away was wearing a blanket and boots sending "electrical impulses into the back, the spine, the muscles," Sonny said. The blanket was kept on for half an hour.

"After they stand there for a while, after you get finished with them, it's like they say, 'Wooo, that feels good,'" said Sonny, sitting in a chair at the end of the barn. "See how quiet he is now. He's resting. When you take that blanket off, he'll lay down and go to sleep. He's enjoying it."

When the blanket and boots were removed, Sonny fed the colt some hay. "He wanted to get my hand," Sonny said with a laugh. "He went for my hand. He's tricky."

Carolyn recalled the message that she had received from a fortune cookie at a Chinese restaurant the previous week: *Life's rewards will be yours.* A gust of wind came through the shedrow, blowing her red hair. "I feel young," the personable Carolyn said. "I think this business keeps you young."

Derby owners are provided a courtesy vehicle to use during their stay in Louisville, and Buck Wheat, director of horsemen's relations, dropped by Barn 42 to take Sonny to the infield to select one. "Honey, pick out a red and yellow one," Carolyn told Sonny as he left. (Her silks are red and gold.) "I've always loved red," she said. "I think it's a happy color."

Shortly before 11:00 A.M., Sonny returned, obviously pleased with himself. As he came around the corner of the barn, he couldn't wait to ask, "What color did you want?"

"I'm afraid to look," Carolyn replied. Seeing that it was a red van (with a gold stripe around the windows), she said: "I don't believe this. Are my requests always filled? I wouldn't believe this in a million years. I was joking. I said, 'I want a red car.' Oh, I think that's hysterical."

Richard Seekman, a security officer at the barn, said, "You know what that means. Everything's come true for you."

"Life's rewards," Carolyn said, smiling contentedly as she recalled those precious words from the fortune cookie.

April 23—Standing at an entrance to Barn 42, Pete Johnson looked up at the sky. A light drizzle was falling at 8:10 A.M.

Skip Away, who was going to work out this morning, was led from his stall at 8:18 A.M. Jockey Shane Sellers was in a tack room, and Sonny offered these instructions: "Let him go as he wants. I'm not going to give you a time. He's going to go nice. He can go real slow or he can go real fast as long as that's what he wants to do. Just sit on him and let him breeze. If you want to let him gallop out a little, you can. We'll come back the first of next week and do something a little sharper with him."

As Skip Away was walked around the barn, Carolyn stood at the door to the tack room and said, "I made a major step. I put a hat on." She was wearing a blue Triple Crown cap.

"You see the difference in him," Sonny said, admiring Skip Away as the colt walked around the barn. "He's got a bounce to his step this morning. He knows he's going to work."

Skip Away was led to the gap near the six-furlong pole. "What he does, he'll do," Sonny said. "Can't get all wound up with this stuff. If you do, you'll go nuts. I'm pretty relaxed. Just hope he comes back good from the work."

The light drizzle kept coming down. "Good luck," Sonny said to Sellers as Skip Away stepped on the sloppy track. Sonny and Carolyn watched the workout from a stand near the gap. Steve Haskin of *Daily Racing Form* joined them. "I don't want to go fast," Sonny said. "Just want to maintain where he's at."

Skip Away broke off for the workout, and shortly he began rounding the far turn and disappeared from Sonny's sight. The next time Sonny saw Skip Away, the colt was galloping out around the clubhouse turn. "He galloped strong," a happy Sonny said. "He doesn't want to pull up—son of a gun. He's enjoying it."

Haskin went down to the clockers' stand to get the time for the workout. Returning, he reported to Sonny that Skip Away had run in 1:01⅗, with a final eighth in 12 seconds.

"Are you kidding me?" Hine asked. "He's unbelievable, isn't he? Did it easy, too." As Skip Away walked up the track and past the stand where Hine was observing him, the trainer said, "He's not even blowing. Just maintain it." Following Skip Away back to the barn, Hine added, "Not blowing. He's an amazing athlete."

April 24—Sonny and Carolyn spent last night at the Campbell House. "I feel very good about everything," Sonny said. "He'll be very tough if he stays like he is."

April 27—"Mother's Day's coming up," Sonny remarked. "My wife said, 'I don't want any jewelry. I want another horse.'"

Sonny noted that Carolyn had looked in trainer D. Wayne Lukas's immaculate tack room at the Downs. "She said, 'Look how neat Wayne's tack room is.' I said, 'Hey, we're gyps. Why should we change now?' You can't take the gyp out of a gyp."

Sonny, chuckling, added, "I said, 'Hey, you forget we raced at Wheeling, Waterford, Timonium.' Boy, I raced at gyp joints. I said, 'Look, honey, you can't take the gyp out of the gyp.' I've been a gyp all of my life. What can I tell you?"

"Indian Charlie" at His Mischievous Best

Two weeks before the Derby, carefree Ed Musselman, better known as "Indian Charlie," the publisher of the

Morning Telegraph, dropped by Sonny's tack room at Keeneland and provided him with some chuckles. One item in that day's *Morning Telegraph* reported:

> Following last Saturday's performance by Skip Away came a not-so-mild case of insomnia for his owner Carolyn Hine. It seems she remembered a Derby Week Gala from the last time her [*sic*] and her husband, Sonny, attended the Derby. This special function, on Derby Week, would require Mrs. Hine's finest evening gown. Her problem was, that this lovely dress did not make the ride to Kentucky. It was in a closet somewhere in Miami. When she told her husband, Sonny of this problem, he could not believe his ears. It was 4:00 A.M. and he had another hour to go before he had to get up. Sonny's response was to tell his wife to go to K-Mart and buy herself anything she needed.

Also in this issue was "Sonny And Carolyn Hine's Derby Week Itinerary," which read:

April 27th—Saturday	Lindy's on Preston Hwy.
April 28th—Sunday	Bob Evans I-264
April 29th—Monday	Open
April 30th—Tuesday	Blue Boar on Eastern Parkway
May 1st—Wednesday	Banquet Table Buffet
May 2nd—Thursday	Taco Tico
May 3rd—Friday	Shoney's Buffet
May 4th—Saturday	White Castles or Pat's Steak House

After reading this prose from "Indian Charlie," Sonny had two words to say: "That's funny."

A week before the Derby, "Indian Charlie" and Ronnie Ebanks, agent for Shane Sellers, were up to some mischief. While D. Wayne Lukas was being interviewed, Ebanks mounted the trainer's pony and Musselman put two Skip Away buttons on the headstall of the bridle. Following the interview, Lukas removed one of the buttons but left on the other.

Later, while on the racetrack, Lukas spotted Hine standing in the trainers' stand near the six-furlong gap, and, wearing a big smile, he rode his pony over to show off the Skip Away button that was still on the headstall. As Lukas rode away, Sonny said, "Everybody's wearing the buttons. Even Lukas has one on his pony. That's funny."

Sunday, April 28—Derby Week, and the countdown continued for the 122nd running of America's most celebrated horse race. Skip Away jogged a mile and one-quarter and galloped a mile and three-eighths. "He's the kind of horse that really thrives on training," Sonny said. "I really think he's coming to the race better than any race we've come to."

Monday, April 29—In the privacy of her tack room, Carolyn talked quietly about how much she wanted Skip Away to win the Derby for Sonny's sake. She spoke about how hard he had worked during his career—seven days a week, always up early in the morning—and how much she wanted him to be rewarded.

Skip Away was to receive his final workout for the Derby this morning. As was the case for his workout the previous week at the Downs, the track was sloppy. "I don't like taking him out in the rain on an off track," Sonny said. "I don't have a choice. You worry."

On his walk around the shedrow, Skip Away was led past Sonny. "Hey, champ," Sonny called to him. It was 8:00 A.M. "I wish it'd stop raining," Sonny said.

The next time the colt came by, Carolyn said, "Hey, Skip."

Sonny gave quick instructions to jockey Shane Sellers, saying, in part, "Go a useful five-eighths. Want him blowing a little bit."

"I got you, I got you," Sellers said.

Before going out for the workout, Sellers told a group of reporters, "I don't think he's run his best race yet. He's coming into the race so good. He's the talk of the backside." Sellers soon was given a leg up by Pete Johnson.

82 DERBY MAGIC

When Sonny arrived in the stand near the six-furlong gap, he looked at the sloppy track and said, "Boy, is that a mess." Skip Away worked five-eighths handily in 1:00²/₅, a bullet move. "That was a good work—on this track," Sonny said.

Back at the barn, Johnson said of the workout, "Love it, love it, love it." After Skip Away cooled off, "he rolled on one side; he rolled on his other side; he got up and squealed," Johnson noted. "It shows that he's a happy horse."

Skip Away, who had bled from both nostrils in a January 10 allowance at Gulfstream Park, was scoped after the workout by veterinarian Rick Fischer. "Clean as a pin," Sonny said.

Tuesday, April 30—Reflecting on Skip Away's Monday workout, Sonny remarked, "I thought he was blowing a little bit. He needed that work."

"He really came out of the work super," said Pete Johnson. "Ate up good last night. In fact, he ate up better last night than he did the night before."

Sonny's twelve horses at Keeneland arrived at Monmouth Park this morning at seven o'clock by van.

Wednesday, May 1—Certain other Derby horses have been grazing at the Downs, but not Skip Away. Sonny was worried about what Skip Away could pick up if a sick horse was grazing in the area. "I know he would love it, but I can't take a chance. I'm a little afraid of it."

Shortly before 3:00 P.M. on this cloudy day, Sonny pulled up at the barn with Carolyn, her brother, Dr. Irving Seaman, and his wife, Bernice, a lovely couple who had just flown in from Florida. Each was wearing a Skip Away button. Sonny introduced them by saying that these are the people who turned down the chance to own part of Skip Away.

To which Bernice said with a smile, "And we're still friends."

The sun finally shone through. "Gee, the sun's out,"

Carolyn said. "What happened? Did somebody put an order in?"

After the group spent a short time at the barn, it was time to go. Sonny lifted a waist-high railing for Carolyn and the others to lean under as they left the barn. Sonny put the railing back. "How do you do the limbo, Bernice?" Sonny asked, acting as if he was going to limbo under the railing.

"He can't do it," Carolyn said.

"He's got one problem," Bernice said of her heavyset brother-in-law.

Sonny was happy as he left the barn, but several hours later the smile was wiped off his face when Skip Away drew the number-seventeen post position for the Kentucky Derby. "I'm very upset," he said at the Sports Spectrum, where the draw was held. "Very, very upset. If I had eight or ten, I'd be very confident." Sonny did manage a smile when he mentioned that Charlie Whittingham, the trainer of Corker, told him: "Don't worry about the post. You got the horse."

Thursday, May 2—Had Sonny recovered from the Derby's draw for post positions? "Yeah, some things we can't control," he replied.

I had spent a month around Sonny and Skip Away, and on this morning I caught the first bad vibes from the stable following a training session. Skip Away wasn't handling the Downs track.

Sonny said the Downs track this morning was laboring. "He was blowing a little bit after his gallop." It was not a good sign—not a good sign at all.

Louisvillian Frank Gitschier, a former FBI man himself, dropped by the barn and was introduced to the trainer. The two of them talked about their days with the bureau. One of Gitschier's sons, Greg, a current FBI agent, also was introduced to Sonny.

"I was really impressed with his down-to-earth approach,"

Frank Gitschier said later that day. "This guy's a human being. He's not trying to impress you. I personally would *love* to see Sonny Hine in the winner's circle. I think he's really a *genuine* person."

Friday, May 3—Skip Away, with exercise rider Jose-Clemente Sanchez up, galloped a mile and five-eighths this morning. "It was beautiful," Sonny said. "He had some jog in him when he came back. He was feeling good."

How did he handle the track? "Between you and me, yesterday he looked terrible over it," Sonny said. "He labored on it. I hope I get a wet-fast track or a fast track. He'd like a fast track."

Inside a tack room, Sonny and jockey Shane Sellers talked about the Derby riding strategy. "You know the gray horse," Sonny told Sellers. "You do it. You're the man."

Would the Third Time Be a Charm for Sonny?

Sonny had started two previous horses in the Derby—Cojak, who finished sixth at 38-1 odds in 1976, and Technology, tenth as the 4.20-1 second choice in 1992. In both years, things weren't going right for the heavy favorite in the days leading up to the Derby. Honest Pleasure finished second as the 2-5 favorite in 1976 and Arazi came in eighth as the 9-10 favorite in 1992.

In 1996, the highly regarded Unbridled's Song developed a foot problem and wasn't heading into the Derby in the most desirable way.

Some observers didn't think Skip Away could duplicate his Blue Grass effort in the Derby, but if he was able to maintain his form, he figured to be a serious contender in the 122nd Run for the Roses.

Where trainer Jim Ryerson was under tremendous pressure with Unbridled's Song, Sonny was quite relaxed as the Derby approached. He had the best of all possible worlds.

His owner wasn't going to fire him. After all, he was married to her.

Asked to compare this Derby to his previous two experiences, Sonny said during Derby Week, "It's my own horse this time. Just doing it for myself this time. What else can I say? My wife and I like it better. I don't have to answer to anybody."

A Hat for a Lovely Woman

Carolyn isn't a hat person but was going to purchase one for the Kentucky Derby. "She looks good in hats," Sonny said. "They told her she should wear a hat out of respect. Everybody told her she should wear a hat. Can't go to the Derby without a hat."

Carolyn purchased two hats for the occasion. "I have two different suits with me," she said. "I'm going to see how the weather is. I love the two hats that I bought"—one beige and the other black.

Carolyn sometimes would appear at the barn wearing a blue Triple Crown cap, but six days before the Derby she received a surprise present from Sonny. Returning from the track that morning, he told her, "Wait till you see these things. I want you to see these hats. Look at these hats, honey." Kathy Garcia, who formerly had ponied horses for Sonny, was selling all kinds of items—horse dolls, caps, and hats.

"I bought two hats already," Carolyn replied.

She then put on a red straw hat. "That's you—that's you, that's you, that's you," assistant trainer Pete Johnson said, smiling and pointing at Carolyn.

"I like that, honey," Sonny agreed.

Carolyn, at the tack-room door, said, "I can't believe I'm standing here with a hat on."

"You look good," Sonny told her. He paid Garcia for the hat. "I like your hat, honey," Sonny told Carolyn.

"I'm not used to hats," she said. This straw hat was decorated with roses around the brim and a horse's head in front with a horse's rear end and tail in the back. Good sport that Carolyn is, she wore the hat that morning.

Saturday, May 4—Derby Day. "I think he'll perform real well," Sonny said this morning. "Just a bad post. Can't make any mistakes." Leaving the barn, Sonny said, "If it's meant to be, it'll be."

A severe overnight thunderstorm, with large hail, had hit the Louisville area, but the Downs racing surface has the remarkable capacity to bounce back—and, thanks to work by the track crew, it was fast for the Derby Day card. Even so, it wasn't to Skip Away's liking. If the Blue Grass was too good to be true, as some suggested, the Derby was too bad to be true for Skip Away. He finished twelfth. Life went on. His people were naturally disappointed, but they maintained a positive attitude that is so prevalent around their barn.

"I'll guarantee you he didn't handle the racetrack," Sonny said. "But we had a gut feeling he wouldn't. He galloped Thursday and was blowing."

Sonny and Carolyn will long remember this Derby experience. And those who met this couple for the first time were quite impressed with their graciousness and goodness.

"It was a great experience," Sonny said in the late afternoon on Derby Day. "The people are unbelievable. They treated us like royalty everywhere we went."

Someone commented to Carolyn that she looked beautiful in her green outfit and black hat.

"She's a beautiful girl—and, believe me, she won't fire me tonight," said Sonny, who couldn't resist adding, "maybe tomorrow morning."

They kissed. "I got the best," Carolyn said. "I don't want the rest." She was appreciating life's *real* rewards.

Preakness Postscript: A Proud Effort at Pimlico

Five days before the Preakness, Skip Away worked five furlongs in an eye-catching fifty-nine seconds at Monmouth
Park, another bullet move. "He was just as awesome as he
was before the Blue Grass," Sonny said shortly after Skip
Away arrived at Pimlico two days before the Preakness. "It
was unbelievable."

The morning before the Preakness, Hine liked what he
saw of Skip Away in his training. "Oh, boy, was he aggressive
this morning," he said. "Very aggressive." At the Alibi
Breakfast that morning, Sonny told the audience, "My wife
said if I wouldn't bring the horse down, the assistant trainer
would. So I'm here."

Twelve horses had been entered in the Preakness, and
once again Skip Away drew one of the outside post positions—eleven. Skip Away was listed at 6-1 in the morning
line but was bet down to 3.30-1 by post time, second choice.

The track was muddy for the first race on the Preakness
card, but as the afternoon wore on, the condition of the racing surface began to improve. Less than three hours before
the Preakness, Pete Johnson stood outside Skip Away's stall
at Pimlico and said, "I feel good. I really feel good. I really
didn't feel good about the Derby. I was hoping for the best,
but I didn't have a really good feeling. But, personally, I
think he'll handle this racetrack.

"I know he's a good horse," the assistant trainer added.
"One race ain't going to make him; one race ain't going to
break him. I still think he's the best horse Sonny's ever
trained. If everything goes right today, he'll show up. He's
doing good."

As someone who had been hanging around the Skip
Away barn for more than a month now, I was sensing good
things. I was convinced Skip Away was going to run his race
in the Preakness. I just didn't know if another horse was
going to run a better race.

As is part of the Preakness tradition, the horses were saddled on the grass course in the infield. Fifteen minutes before post time, Shane Sellers put his arm around Johnson and gave him a hug. After Sellers was given a leg up by Johnson, Carolyn said, "Come on, Skip. You can do it, baby." Sellers waved to Carolyn. "Good luck, Shane," she said to him.

Louis Quatorze, who broke from the number-six post, took the lead early in the race and stayed in front the entire way to win the 1³/₁₆-mile classic in 1:53²/₅, equaling the stakes record on a track that was fast for the Preakness. Skip Away ran well himself, finishing second, 3¼ lengths behind the winner. Skip Away made a move coming into the homestretch, and for a moment it appeared to me that he was going to overtake Louis Quatorze. But Louis Quatorze was stronger in the run through the homestretch and was pulling away at the finish.

Back at the barn, Sonny said, "Not taking anything away from the winner, but change the post positions and a little better luck, we'd have gotten the money." In summation, he remarked, "He ran a good race. I was very proud of him."

Belmont: Even in Defeat, a Beauty of a Race

On June 2, six days before the Belmont Stakes, Skip Away drilled seven furlongs in 1:25⅕ at Monmouth Park, a move that delighted Hine. "He worked dynamite," Hine said. "He's in excellent shape. We scoped him, and we were pleased that he scoped good."

For the Belmont, Skip Away again drew an outside post position—thirteen in the field of fourteen. First, he wound up starting from the sixteenth spot in the Derby after one of the entrants was withdrawn, and then he had the number-eleven post in the Preakness. His three post positions in the Triple Crown races added up to forty. The day before the Belmont, Hine, always the comedian, said from his barn at

Hubert ("Sonny") Hine, trainer of Skip Away, talked with jockey Shane Sellers at the 1996 Preakness Stakes at Pimlico. (Photo by Jim Bolus)

Skip Away prior to the Preakness Stakes. (Photo by Jim Bolus)

Monmouth Park, "Well, I see Skip Away got his lucky number thirteen in the post draw. Actually, it was the first time Skip Away spoke to me by saying he was happy he didn't get post sixteen [which he had in the Derby]."

Skip Away ran a game race in the Belmont. Those who doubted his distance ability should have looked at the teletimer when he led after a mile and one-quarter in 2:02. They should have checked Skip Away out at the eighth pole, when he still led by a half-length. Editor's Note passed him, but Skip Away came back to edge ahead. Nearing the finish, Editor's Note regained the lead and went on to win by a length over runner-up Skip Away.

Afterward, Hine said, "You only have one chance to go through something like this [running in the Triple Crown]. It's unfortunate my horse had to draw outside posts in each race. Each time you draw the outside, you have to use more horse to get position. He ran very hard today. He broke a step slow, and he had to be used hard to clear seven or eight other horses to get position. We were just outrun in the end.

"He has more ability than his father, Skip Trial," Hine added. "He's very agile. I'm going to take him back to Monmouth Park, give him a rest, and get him ready for the Haskell and Travers. That's the route we plan to take. Hopefully, we will get a better post in those races."

Claude R. ("Shug") McGaughey III, trainer of Belmont third-place finisher My Flag, paid Skip Away a nice compliment afterward. Jennie Rees of *The Courier-Journal* quoted him as saying of the three-year-olds, "I think they're a nice bunch of horses. There sure isn't a superstar. But you'd have to think Skip Away is a pretty good horse. Three out of his last four races have been great races. He was up in the running of that race [the Belmont] the whole way, and that was a pretty grueling racetrack. He's going to be tough in some of these races down the road."

Skip Away was tough in the races down the road. He won the Ohio Derby, the Buick Haskell Invitational Handicap,

Carolyn Hine, owner of Skip Away, had plenty of reasons to smile during her colt's championship season of 1996. (Photo by Jim Bolus)

the Woodbine Million, the 1¼-mile Jockey Club Gold Cup in 2:00⅗ (defeating the celebrated Cigar) and earned the Eclipse Award as champion three-year-old colt. The award couldn't have gone to two finer people, Carolyn and Sonny Hine. Thanks for the memories.

Tex Sutton, a household name in the field of transporting horses, is shown in his earlier days loading a horse on a train. (Photo courtesy Skeets Meadors)

8

Up, Up, and Away

As HIS HORSES were being led onto a 727 in the early-morning hours of October 24, 1995, trainer D. Wayne Lukas said with a smile: "I don't know if we're going to have filet and lobster today. We might have cold sandwiches."

Billy Reed, another writer, and I were permitted to join this flight of Lukas horses, leaving Louisville for New York and the Breeders' Cup Championship program that would take place four days later. We weren't served filet and lobster, but it was an experience that beat any visit to a five-star restaurant that I've ever made. I'll always remember this flight, my first with racehorses.

And keep in mind that these weren't just average racehorses. They were special runners from Lukas's championship stable. The plane we were on could carry up to eighteen horses, but it was occupied on this flight by only eight—seven who would run in the Breeders' Cup and stable pony Spud. The seven were Serena's Song, who would win the Eclipse Award as champion three-year-old filly of 1995; Golden Attraction, who would be honored as the best two-year-old filly in North America; Cara Rafaela, destined to run second in the Breeders' Cup Juvenile Fillies; Tipically Irish, another two-year-old filly; and three 1996 Kentucky Derby nominees who would run two-three-four in the Breeders' Cup Juvenile—Hennessy, Editor's Note, and Honour and Glory.

Two of those Derby nominees—Editor's Note and Honour and Glory—ran for the roses in 1996. They lost that race, but Editor's Note did come back to capture the Belmont Stakes. There's an old saying that trainers like to use around the racetrack: "Keep yourself in the best of company and your horses in the worst." With two eventual champions on that plane and three prospects for the 1996 Derby, *I* undoubtedly was in the best of company.

Lukas and his horses have flown thousands of miles with the H. E. Sutton Forwarding Company. "We've carried you farther than your mother did," Sutton foreman Mel Prince told Lukas shortly before takeoff.

With Lukas training them, the horses are always in the

Mel Prince, foreman for the H. E. Sutton Forwarding Company, is an expert in transporting horses. "Our first priority is the horse," he said. "He's our most important thing. Getting there safe is our main objective." (Photo by Jim Bolus)

best of hands. And now that they were on the plane, they were still in the best of hands, with Sutton's expert crew in charge. "These guys are pros," Lukas said. "They're good horsemen besides knowing their plane. It's absolutely to the letter."

The door to the plane was closed at 6:48 A.M. "They're going to fly well," Lukas said soon after the plane took off.

Partitions were set up to form solid stalls for the horses. A first-time passenger on a horse flight observes that there are no windows in the fuselage. Heavy flashes of light could upset the horses, so the windowless fuselage helps make for a calmer flight. We were told to dress warmly for the occasion because the temperature on these flights is kept around sixty to sixty-five degrees for the benefit of the horses. "It's just right for a horse," Prince said.

Of the seven racehorses, Golden Attraction was the one who could get stirred up the most, but she was a perfect lady on the trip. With a groom or flight attendant holding a shank on each horse, all seven Thoroughbreds stood quietly in their stalls the entire flight, occasionally munching on hay and acting as if they were back in their cozy Churchill Downs stalls instead of flying thousands of miles in the air on their way to New York.

Lukas said the vast majority of horses aren't sedated before flights because if they have a race coming up in a short time, the medication would show up in a postrace test. "They have medication on board, and if a horse becomes unruly, they'll sedate him," Lukas said. "It's happened on two occasions to me where a horse going to a race became unruly, they sedated it on the airplane, and we had to scratch the horse upon arrival."

Serena's Song was described by Lukas as "probably the most frequently flown horse in the world" in 1995. In order to accomplish what she did on the racetrack, Serena's Song had to pile up the air miles. She started her three-year-old season on the West Coast before coming east. Her travelogue for her thirteen-race campaign showed three starts at Santa Anita Park, followed by one at Turfway, one at Churchill Downs (the Kentucky Derby), one at Pimlico, two at Belmont, one at Monmouth Park, one at Belmont, one at Turfway, and then two more at Belmont. She was tough and she was a champion, ranking among the best—and most valuable—runners in North America.

"As the pilot climbed to his cruising altitude," Reed would write in the *Lexington Herald-Leader*, "we tried to guess the value of our four-legged passengers. Somebody tossed out the figure of $36 million, which sounded reasonable."

I heard that we were approaching New York, but with no windows, there was no way of knowing when we were landing. I've traveled many times by air, but when we touched down at JFK International, it was the smoothest landing of any flight I've ever been on.

The plane landed at 8:43 A.M., the actual flying time lasting an hour and forty-five minutes. Upon arriving at the airport, the horses were led onto two vans and transported directly to the racetrack. A person going by commercial flight would have had to go through the airport, battle crowds, and deal with New York traffic before arriving at Belmont Park, but there were no such worries for the horses. They traveled in style, thanks to the Sutton crew that has this business down to a science. "It was very uneventful, and it was very, very easy for them," Lukas said after the vans arrived at Belmont at 9:48. "That's about as good as they ship—every one of them."

The flight cost more than $20,000, but the Lukas horses more than paid their way. Although none of them won on the Breeders' Cup Championship card, they collectively brought home $716,000 in purses for their efforts on this rich afternoon of racing. A person could buy plenty of filet and lobster with that kind of a payoff.

Old-timers from the 1800s and early 1900s would never

have believed this modern-day phenomenon of air transportation for horses. Let's take a look at some historical milestones.

The First Flights

The transporting of horses by air goes back to at least 1928, the year that Phantom was flown over the English Channel in a French plane. However, it wasn't until after World War II that the racing industry began seriously to look to the skies as a means of transporting horses.

On October 22, 1945, when El Lobo and Featherfoot were sent from Hollywood Park to the Bay Meadows track in Northern California, it was believed to be the first time Thoroughbreds were flown from one meeting to another. A caption under a photograph in *The Blood-Horse* magazine said, "The two horses were led from the van directly into the rear door of the plane, going up the sharply tilted ramp without resistance. They made the trip without incident, went to sleep on the way."

A story by R. E. Leighninger in *The Blood-Horse* said of the horses' arrival at 1:08 P.M. that day, "Boom—heavy bump . . . El Lobo bounces up . . . Steady in an instant . . . We taxi . . .

"Ramps open . . . 5,000 people outside . . . cops busy . . . flashlights, cameras . . . people . . . We're in front of Bay Meadows grandstand . . . The horses unload without a false step . . . then pose for camera . . . led to paddock 50 feet away."

After examining El Lobo and Featherfoot, track veterinarian Dr. L. J. Cook wrote the following report:

> I have inspected both horses . . . less than 10 minutes after landing. I find both to be absolutely normal in every respect, pulse and temperature. They are in perfect condition. I am amazed for this rarely happens after shipment of any other nature.

Leighninger concluded his story writing that the two horses "could have raced that afternoon."

Five days later, El Lobo did race at Bay Meadows—and he won the Burlingame Handicap. "He flew up there, and he flew when he got there," said Stuart Hamblen, the owner of El Lobo.

The following year, six horses became the first to make the flight from Ireland to California. A specially outfitted DC-4 of the American Overseas Airline was used for the flight. Total elapsed time of the trip was thirty-five hours and nineteen minutes; total flying time, thirty hours and forty-five minutes. "Trans-ocean shipment of six Irish Thoroughbreds to Santa Anita Park by fast airliner—the first such aerial cargo in history," *The Blood-Horse* reported. "The highly successful shipment points to a new era on the Turf, with observers foreseeing aerial transportation of Thoroughbreds for classic race engagements in Europe, South America, Australia, and the United States in the immediate future."

In time, flying horses around the globe did become commonplace in the racing world. For example, English and French horses were flown to New York in the fall of 1995 for the Breeders' Cup and supporting stakes that weekend. The flight carrying nine horses from France lasted about seven and a half hours.

In the old days, a trip across the Atlantic took quite a bit more time. When 1935 Triple Crown champion Omaha left New York for England by boat in 1936, it required seven days, not seven hours.

On Trust First Derby Horse to
Come in "on Wings"

In 1947, On Trust made history by being the first Derby horse flown to Louisville. The headline over an April 21, 1947 story spread across the top of a page in *The Louisville*

Times announced the West Coast horse's invasion: "On Trust Arrives Okeh As First Derby Hope to Come In On Wings." Buck Weaver wrote:

> [On Trust] got his first smell of Kentucky air as the four-engine American Air Lines transport carrying him and his entourage got the range over Standiford Field at 7. Fifteen minutes later the plane had landed, just eight hours and twenty minutes after the take-off last night from Long Beach, Calif. Except for the low ceiling encountered here, and it didn't seem to bother Capt. C.A. Lippincott and First Officer J.P. Cole too much as they made a perfect landing, flying conditions were ideal for the cross country trip. Only one stop was made en route, that at Tulsa for refueling. In every respect the trans-continental trip was uneventful. On Trust, according to Trainer Willie Molter, took the flight with the grace of an air pilot and seemed none the worse from the experience.

A jacked-up platform was used to remove On Trust from the plane. "We did have the very devil of a time unloading, for there were no air transport facilities then at the airport," Clyde Turk, assistant trainer for On Trust, once recalled. "They put a hoist truck up beside the plane, built a temporary enclosure around the hoist platform, and somehow we got off the plane safely."

Flying Became the Way to Travel

In 1947, most of the Derby horses brought to Louisville traveled by railway. A story that I wrote in 1968 noted times had changed since On Trust's trip. Ten of the fourteen starters in the 1968 Derby came to Kentucky by air. The other four were vanned here.

The only transporting mishap among the fourteen starters in 1968 occurred not by air but by van. A van carrying Captain's Gig from South Carolina caught fire in the

Smoky Mountains. Captain's Gig had to jump off the truck to escape injury.

Joe Tronzo, an agent for Van Gorp Van Service in Louisville, estimated in 1968 that trucks did 98 percent of the shipping of horses. "Railroads used to be number one," he said at the time. "But highways and airlines have just about run the railroad out of the horse transportation business."

Danger Sometimes in the Air

On rare occasions, the skies are not so friendly for racehorses. The first equine casualty in horse air transportation "was reported in 1947, when a Mexican racehorse, Joselito, became upset and kicked himself to death," Deirdre Biles wrote in the May 6, 1995 issue of *The Blood-Horse*. "In 1951, a Peruvian racehorse, Canastos, was shot twice in the head by a pilot when the animal threatened to damage the plane's fuselage with his kicking. Canastos survived the ordeal, despite profuse bleeding."

Johnny McCabe, who pioneered the business of flying horses around the country in the 1940s, was quoted in a 1963 *Sports Illustrated* article as saying, "In my very first year, a crack French stallion named Djelal, bought for the stud by an American syndicate headed by A. B. Hancock, Jr., for $250,000, went wild in a plane about an hour out of Orly Field, Paris. The horse started kicking in panic and broke a left foreleg on the side of a huge box. By the time the plane got to London, poor Djelal was dead [shot in flight]. The horse undoubtedly had been panicked by the continued barking of some forty K-9 police dogs being returned on the same plane by the U.S. Army.

"But on the whole we have been very lucky. I have had just one horse go berserk in fifteen years. This was a yearling, one of a shipment of twelve, which went wild on a flight and had to be destroyed by the captain so that the rest of them wouldn't be panicked."

In a 1995 *Thoroughbred Times* story, author Dr. Franco Varola wrote that he remembered only two cases of horses who had to be shot in flight "because of untreatable craziness"—Djelal and the Brazilian Canavial, who was en route to Chile.

A United Press International story in 1966 said that several years earlier "a plane carrying eight Peruvian Thoroughbreds was forced to crash land in an isolated valley in Argentina." The crewmen and horses were safe, "but by the time a military rescue party reached the group, they had slaughtered—and eaten—one of the Thoroughbreds."

Isaac Murphy. (Photo courtesy Keeneland Library)

9

Honest Ike

IN THE NINETEENTH CENTURY, black jockeys were ever present on American racetracks. Fourteen of the fifteen riders in the inaugural Kentucky Derby of 1875 were black. Fifteen of the first twenty-eight Derbies were won by black jockeys. But the last black jockey to win the Derby was Jimmy Winkfield, in 1902, and the last to ride in the race was Henry King, in 1921.

Several factors have led to the virtual disappearance of black riders. Discrimination no doubt played a role, and some insist that blacks today are generally not small enough to meet jockey weight requirements. Moreover, blacks don't have as much exposure to the profession as they once did. In the nineteenth century, many grew up on, or around, plantations and farms, and it was only natural that a percentage would learn to ride horses and become jockeys.

One such black who grew up in the horse-racing country of central Kentucky was Isaac Murphy, arguably the best jockey of that century, black or white.

At the time of his death, in 1896, a newspaper obituary suggested that "Honest Isaac" would serve as an appropriate epitaph for Murphy. Honesty and integrity, indeed, were his hallmarks. Murphy once advised a fellow rider with a shady reputation, "You just ride to win. They get you to pull a horse in a selling race, and when it comes to a stake race, they get Isaac to ride. A jockey that'll sell out to one man will sell out to another. Just be honest and you'll have no trouble and plenty of money."

Murphy practiced what he preached. He was as honest as they came, and his reputation was known throughout the racing world. Turfman L. P. Tarlton paid Murphy the following tribute after the jockey's death:

> So well recognized was it that Isaac could not be cor-
> rupted, that very few had the temerity to ever suggest
> wrong-doing to him, and whenever he had the least
> suspicion he would simply return the colors and refuse
> to ride. On one or two occasions he was put on a "dead
> one." The first time he vented his indignation on the
> horse and punished it so severely as to destroy its
> future usefulness. This he ever afterward referred to
> with regret if not mortification. In the other cases he
> boldly notified the judges of his suspicions.

Despite his integrity in the saddle, Murphy's career was not without controversy, due to several accusations of riding while intoxicated. It seems that Murphy was plagued by a weight problem for most of his career, and when wasted from reducing, he would drink champagne to perk himself up. Even though this problem led to some trouble on the track, his legacy to racing is that of a scrupulously honest jockey, one who rode to win.

Murphy won many major races during his remarkable twenty-one-year riding career. He triumphed in three runnings of the Kentucky Derby, a record that wasn't equaled until 1930 and wasn't broken until 1948. In addition, he won the Latonia Derby (called the Hindoo Stakes for three of those runnings) five times, the Clark Stakes four times in Louisville, and the American Derby on four occasions (including the first three) in Chicago. Murphy rode three of those American Derby winners for owner E. J. ("Lucky") Baldwin, who paid the jockey handsomely for his services—$10,000 annually to guarantee first call. During his peak years, Murphy was reported to have earned $15,000 to $20,000.

He was worth every nickel of the money. This soft-spoken jockey who stood about five feet tall was a giant of the racing world. He possessed a sixth sense when it came to riding horses. Instead of indiscriminately punishing his horses with whip and spur, Murphy preferred to use his head and gentle hands in order to get the most from his mounts. A great judge of pace, he liked to play it close, and frequently he'd ask his mounts to put forth just enough effort to win. Those tight finishes came to be known as "Murfinishes."

The only person I've ever interviewed who saw the long-armed Murphy ride was Nate Cantrell, a black man who was still active as a trainer at the age of ninety-six in 1975. "I seen Isaac Murphy ride when he was comin' in such a close finish when he had to take his whip and put his whip under the chin of a horse and make him throw his head up to win," Cantrell told me. "He was just that way. I saw him ride, oh, I couldn't tell you how many races I seen him ride. I know him personally. He didn't have two words to say to nobody. Everything about him was a gentleman."

Murphy, indeed, would have been a modern-day public relations person's dream. *I Like Ike* buttons would have appeared for this admired jockey long before Dwight ever came along. Murphy's exploits as a jockey were so legendary that he was called "the colored Archer," a reference to the famous English jockey, Fred Archer. Some observers thought this wording was reversed, that Archer actually could have been referred to as "the white Murphy."

Murphy turned down a large inducement to compete in England "because it would be a disadvantage to any horse I rode, for they combine against our white jockeys over there and they would beat any horse I rode sure."

Murphy, a native of Kentucky, was born the son of James Burns, a freeman and bricklayer who had enlisted in the Union forces and died in a Confederate prison camp during the Civil War.

When Murphy began exercising horses at the age of twelve or thirteen, he weighed just seventy pounds. Taught the art of riding by noted black trainer "Uncle Eli" Jordan, he launched his career on May 22, 1875, at the inaugural meeting of the Louisville Jockey Club (the official name of Churchill Downs in those days). His first victory came the following year, on September 15, when he rode Glentina, a two-year-old filly carrying eighty-seven pounds, to victory at the Kentucky Association track in Lexington. In the early part of his career, he weighed just seventy-four pounds and rode as Isaac Burns.

By the time he rode in his first Kentucky Derby (1877), he had assumed the surname of his grandfather, Green Murphy, at his mother's request. Murphy, who finished fourth on Vera Cruz in that Derby, always thought he would have won if his mount had gotten off to a good start. Later that fall in Louisville, he won his first major stakes, the St. Leger, aboard Vera Cruz.

Murphy was off and running. In 1884, he swept the three most important races at the Churchill Downs spring meeting—the Kentucky Derby and Clark Stakes with Buchanan and the Kentucky Oaks with Modesty. Actually, Murphy didn't want to ride Buchanan in the Derby. Buchanan was considered a rogue, a horse who would act up on the track, in the saddling area, or almost anyplace. He had the reputation of being one of the wildest Thoroughbreds in America.

Murphy had signed a contract with owner Capt. William Cottrill to ride Buchanan in the Derby, but as the race approached the jockey was trying to back out of his commitment. Buchanan's people, however, refused to allow Murphy a mount in the Derby if he didn't ride their colt. They told track officials of their feeling, and the judges ruled that he would have to ride Buchanan in the Derby—or no horse at all. Faced with the possibility of being suspended for the entire meeting, Murphy took the mount and brought Buchanan, a maiden, home a winner.

In 1889, Murphy was asked to name the best horse he ever rode. He mentioned the names of Freeland, Leonatus,

Checkmate, and others, but then settled on Emperor of Norfolk, a future Hall of Famer who starred in 1887 and 1888. "I tell you he was a wonder," Murphy said, "and when in the best of condition I have yet to see the horse that, in my opinion, could defeat him."

It was aboard Emperor of Norfolk, however, that he experienced some bad publicity. Following an unsatisfactory ride aboard that colt in an 1887 race at Monmouth, Murphy was accused of drinking champagne. A publication known as *The Spirit of the Times* declared:

> All jockeys drink champagne. It often forms their only stimulant of victuals and drink when they are reducing. But we saw as much and maybe more of Murphy and we failed to perceive any intoxication.

The Gay Nineties brought Murphy the best of times—and the worst of times. He won his last two Kentucky Derbies in 1890, with Riley, and 1891, with Kingman. Following his victory aboard Riley, *The Courier-Journal* referred to Murphy as "a quiet, polite young man, who never made a bet in his life, never swore and never was caught telling a lie. His integrity and honor are the pride of the turf, and many of the best horsemen pronounce him the greatest jockey that ever mounted a horse. His face, like a Sphinx carved out of mahogany, is familiar on every race track in America."

On June 25, 1890, Murphy rode Salvator to a match-race victory over Tenny. Murphy was riding high, having won the Kentucky Derby that year and this celebrated match race, but two months later he suffered a severe blow to his reputation when he finished out of the money aboard the favored Firenze in the Monmouth Handicap. Murphy, dizzy and swaying, nearly fell off Firenze several times during the race and did topple off afterward. He "acted in such a dazed, blinded way that it gave considerable foundation for the rumor that he had been drugged," *The Spirit of the Times* reported. "It is to be presumed that the unholy mixture of milk-punch, Apollinaris and ginger ale, to which Murphy acknowledges, is responsible for the attack of vertigo, which, according to his own account, was so intense that he had the greatest difficulty in keeping his seat during the race, and did not know his own valet in the paddock."

Charged with drunkenness, he was suspended by the judges for an unsatisfactory ride. The tearful Murphy said that he wasn't intoxicated but was weak from reducing and was suffering a severe attack of dizziness. Speculation also surfaced that he had been drugged, a contention that Murphy himself later believed.

The New York Times saw fit to print a story ripping Murphy for his performance. "A popular idol was shattered at Monmouth Park yesterday," the newspaper reported. "That Isaac Murphy, who has always been considered the most gentlemanly as well as the most honest of jockeys, should have made such an exhibition of himself as he did was past belief. . . . Murphy's disgraceful exhibition was due to overindulgence in champagne, a habit which has in times past gotten the better of him, but never to lead to quite so sad an exhibition of himself as he made on the track yesterday."

It was said that Murphy, one of the best-liked jockeys of his day, never got over the incident, that his popularity as a rider declined afterward, but in 1891 he did win thirty-two races, including his third Kentucky Derby. However, he was unable to maintain top form the rest of his career. Murphy won only six races in 1892 and four in 1893. He was winless with seven mounts in 1894, a year in which he was temporarily suspended for allegedly being drunk while riding a horse named Myrtle II. The next year, Murphy triumphed just twice in twenty rides. On November 13, 1895, at the Kentucky Association track, he rode for the last time, and he went out a winner aboard a fainthearted 8-1 shot named Tupto. One account said Murphy "nursed that famous quitter and landed him a winner."

Murphy, who retired after the 1895 season, fought such a weight battle that in the off-seasons he would balloon to between 130 and 140 pounds. One 1882 account said he had become seriously ill due to a severe strain after reducing to riding weight.

Unlike all too many old-time jockeys who squandered their money, the sensible Murphy was careful with his. In the late 1880s, he built a home described as an "elegant residence" overlooking the historic Kentucky Association track's backstretch. He also owned a small string of racehorses.

By Murphy's own records, he triumphed aboard 628 of his 1,412 mounts, an incredible success rate of 45 percent. It's questionable whether his percentage was actually that good, because according to racing guides of the time and other sources, he won with something like 33 percent of his mounts. Still, that was a brilliant record, considering that Eddie Arcaro, regarded as the greatest twentieth-century jockey in America by some longtime observers, had a winning rate of 20 percent.

Murphy hadn't been in good health near the end of his career, and less than a year after he retired, he came down with pneumonia. Early in the evening of February 11, 1896, his wife called a doctor, and soon after midnight on February 12, Murphy died. Accounts have varied regarding his age, but he most likely was thirty-five. On a snowy Sunday, February 16, more than five hundred people, including some of racing's most distinguished personalities, attended his funeral, which some people claimed was the largest ever held in Lexington. The services took place at his home. "The Lexington Choral Club sang several touching funeral songs," *The Courier-Journal* reported, "and the body was escorted from the house to the cemetery by Bethany Commandery Knights Templar. . . . Floral tributes were sent from nearly everywhere, it requiring a large wagon to haul all the flowers that the dead jockey's admirers had sent to decorate his grave. The remains were buried in the colored cemetery on Seventh street, one of the most beautiful spots around Lexington."

Murphy was interred in Lexington No. 2 Cemetery, with a wooden cross marking his grave. The cross rotted, and years later, in 1909, friends erected a more suitable marker, one made of concrete. However, the once-beautiful cemetery in time was abandoned, and Murphy's grave was overgrown with vines and weeds.

Thanks to the effort of Lexington journalist Frank Borries, Jr., Murphy's long-neglected grave was found, and in 1967 the jockey's remains were reinterred in a place of honor at the Man o' War Park, Lexington, near the grave of the legendary racehorse Man o' War. Some ten years later, Murphy's remains and those of Man o' War were reburied at the Kentucky Horse Park, near Lexington. The marker over this jockey's grave stands there for thousands of visitors to see each year as they stroll through the Kentucky Horse Park in the heart of the Bluegrass State, where "Honest Isaac" was born and died.

10

Clyde Van Dusen Was a "Mud-Runnin' Fool"

JOCKEY LINUS ("PONY") MCATEE HAD a blind date for the 1929 Kentucky Derby. It was with Clyde Van Dusen, a horse the rider had never seen before he climbed aboard him for this race.

Clyde Van Dusen, a son of Man o' War, was a small horse—so small, in fact, that his trainer made a special trip to the jockeys' room before the Derby to tell McAtee not to let his heart sink or be discouraged over the horse's diminutiveness.

"He can't be small enough to surprise me," McAtee assured the trainer, Clyde Van Dusen, for whom the horse was named. "I've ridden some mighty little horses."

Even though warned, McAtee was shocked when he arrived at the paddock and got his first glimpse of Clyde Van Dusen.

But Clyde Van Dusen stood tall on May 18, 1929, when he won the fifty-fifth running of the Kentucky Derby. Finishing fourth in the race was Blue Larkspur, the best horse ever owned by the famous Col. E. R. Bradley. Blue Larkspur had an excuse for his loss. Because of the track's deplorable muddy condition, he needed new shoes, but he never did get them.

A rain on Derby morning didn't put a damper on Bradley's hopes for Blue Larkspur. "Blue Larkspur can run as well in the mud as on the dry," Bradley said, "and I do

111

Linus ("Pony") McAtee, the jockey on 1929 Kentucky Derby winner Clyde Van Dusen. (Photo courtesy Keeneland-Cook)

not believe any change in track conditions would seriously affect his chances."

Those backing Clyde Van Dusen welcomed the rain. As a matter of fact, back at Few Acres Farm near Lexington where the horse was foaled, some black workers had prayed Derby morning for rain.

Their prayers were answered. The downpour became heavier, and, before it was over, a total of 1.19 inches of rain fell on Derby Day. The track, a sea of mud, was so bad that it was a sound idea for the horses to be shod with mud caulks in order for them to get a better hold of the racing surface.

But in the absence of trainer H. J. ("Derby Dick") Thompson, who was hospitalized with appendicitis, the Bradley stable was in disarray. When a member of the stable attempted to have Blue Larkspur reshod, he was brushed aside by a blacksmith, who said the horse didn't need mud caulks. Blue Larkspur consequently ran with slick shoes in the Derby.

Blue Larkspur entered the Derby with a record of five triumphs in eight starts. In his only 1929 Derby prep, he edged Clyde Van Dusen by a neck in a race of a mile and seventy yards at Lexington.

In the Derby, Blue Larkspur was coupled with Bay Beauty, the Bradley entry being favored at 1.71-1. (Churchill Downs paid off to the penny at that time.) Clyde Van Dusen was the 3-1 second choice.

The '29 Derby was the last renewal to use the web barrier as the method of starting the horses. The horses would line up with their heads touching a net webbing that stretched across the track. When the starter was satisfied with the way the horses were standing, he released the webbing, sending it up and away—and the field would be off and running. The field of twenty-one was at the post thirteen minutes for the '29 Derby before starter Bill Hamilton sent the horses on their way.

Clyde Van Dusen was slated to start from the number-twenty post position. Blue Larkspur had the extreme outside number-twenty-one post. Some believed that, in the long wait, McAtee maneuvered his mount closer to the inside. "Starter Hamilton had considerable trouble in obtaining alignment to his liking," stated one account, "and it was observed that McAtee moved over with Clyde Van Dusen from his assigned position next to the outside in the field of 21 that raced, until he had the son of Man o' War about in the middle of the course, a decided advantage."

A good many witnesses discounted this story, but they didn't have the advantage of looking at the film of the race. All they saw was a stampede of twenty-one horses breaking from the web barrier, and it's doubtful that any of them could tell for sure the exact positioning of Clyde Van Dusen at the start. An inspection of the film of the race indicates that Clyde Van Dusen indeed did start somewhere closer to the middle of the pack instead of from the number-twenty post.

With the inimitable Clem McCarthy broadcasting to r-r-racing fans in the Derby's first worldwide radio hookup, Clyde Van Dusen went to the lead early in the race. The farther they went, the better McAtee was getting to know this little horse. "We had not gone farther than the first turn until I realized I had a good horse under me," McAtee would say afterward.

Blue Larkspur, on the other hand, wasn't striding freely and did a lot of sliding around. Clyde Van Dusen maintained his lead and came splattering home two lengths ahead in the extremely slow time of 2:10⅘. The winner's time for the final quarter of a mile was a full 28 seconds. Blue Larkspur trailed by five lengths at the finish.

"I was kinda scared when I first saw Clyde because he is so little," McAtee said afterward, "but now I can say he is one of the finest and gamest horses of them all. Oh, boy, how he can run! He is nothing but a mud-runnin' fool!"

This was the second Derby victory for McAtee, who won the 1927 renewal with Whiskery. Not only was McAtee a fine jockey, but he was a talented golfer who could shoot in the low 70s and frequently joined Babe Ruth on the links.

Clyde Van Dusen's breeder and owner, Herbert P. Gardner of Amsterdam, New York, didn't attend the Derby because he feared the excitement of the day might be too much for him. Van Dusen, the trainer, accepted the trophy on behalf of Gardner.

"Clyde is a little horse, and that is why Mr. Gardner named him after me," said Van Dusen, a small man who was once a jockey. "I told everybody before the race that I had no excuses to offer for my horse whether he won or lost. It makes no difference to him what the condition of the track is. He just needs room to run."

Meanwhile, back at Few Acres Farm, the farm help was jubilant. John Dishman, a groom at the farm, walked over to the horse's mother, Uncle's Lassie, and raised her head from the grass. "Come here, honey. You're famous now. Let me tell you what your little son did this afternoon."

A visitor asked, "Wouldn't she be proud if she knew that she was the mother of a Derby winner?"

"Why, of course, she knows," John replied. "Didn't you just hear me tell her?"

Dishman helped raise Clyde Van Dusen. "He was the playfullest thing you ever seen," he said. "Just as frisky as he could be, but not mean. Just give him a little piece of sugar and he would follow you all over the farm."

While the Clyde Van Dusen people celebrated, the Bradley stable felt the sting of the Derby defeat. Bradley, a legendary gambler who was reported to have lost $125,000 in bets on the 1929 Derby, made some disparaging remarks about Clyde Van Dusen and Blue Larkspur that were totally out of character for this sportsman. He said Clyde Van Dusen was the worst Derby winner in twenty years. Somewhat embarrassed by the loss, Bradley also said, "I really think I could ride Bubbling Over [his 1926 Derby winner] and beat Blue Larkspur."

Mack Garner, who rode Blue Larkspur for the first time in the 1929 Derby, blamed the loss on the track's condition. "Blue Larkspur will not run his best on a wet track," the jockey said. "I knew he would not win after the first half-mile. He had a tendency to lug in on the rail, all the way, where the going was the worst. He also slipped and seemed to be fighting for a toehold most of the journey. Blue Larkspur is a good, game colt and will take a lot of beating under other conditions. He probably would have won had the course been fast. Dick Thompson had Blue Larkspur in tiptop condition, and all I can say is that no horse in the country can beat Clyde Van Dusen over a heavy track from one jump to the Rocky Mountains."

Others also thought that Blue Larkspur couldn't handle the mud, but such wasn't the case. Shod properly, he could run well in the mud. Blue Larkspur won the 1929 Belmont Stakes on a sloppy track and the Arlington Classic in heavy going.

Clyde Van Dusen finished third in the Arlington Classic, 7½ lengths behind Blue Larkspur. Although Blue Larkspur held a 2-1 edge in meetings with Clyde Van Dusen, the latter's trainer believed he had a better horse. Van Dusen was eager to run his horse against Blue Larkspur and spoke of betting his own money on the outcome of such a race. But they never met again, and Blue Larkspur finished 1929 regarded as the best horse of the year. Not only was he a great racehorse, but he proved to be a prominent sire.

Clyde Van Dusen, a gelding, wasn't the same horse later in his career that he was on Derby Day. He suffered an ignominious fall from glory. Once a stakes winner, he completed his career unable even to capture a claiming race.

There was a reason for the horse's decline, according to John Dishman, the man who raised Clyde Van Dusen. "Mr. Van was working him one day," Dishman recalled many years later, "and he bit the pony Mr. Van was riding. And the old pony kicked him on the inside of his leg. It just swolled up on him, and he never did do no good after that."

Clyde Van Dusen won only one time in 1930, and after sitting out 1931 and 1932, he returned to action in 1933. By that time, Van Dusen owned the gelding. In 1933, Clyde Van Dusen ran ten times, each a claiming race. He failed to win any of those ten. In his final career start, he finished fourth, earning $15—a far cry from the $53,950 he had picked up for his Derby victory.

Clyde Van Dusen subsequently returned to Few Acres Farm, living a life of leisure. He grew heavier but stayed as frisky as ever. A companion of his in those days was an old pony named Bill or Pony Bill, the same lead pony who accompanied Clyde Van Dusen during his racing days.

After the old pony died, Clyde Van Dusen returned to the track—as a pony himself. The '29 Derby winner went back to the racetrack in California as Van Dusen's personal mount, leading the horses the trainer had in his string to the track in the mornings.

Apparently no record was ever made of the death of Clyde Van Dusen. Like an old soldier, this little horse with the king-sized heart just faded into obscurity.

Gallant Fox, with Earl Sande up. (Photo courtesy Keeneland-Cook)

11

The 1930 Derby Was a Landmark, and Gallant Fox Was the Hero

THE KENTUCKY DERBY, A RACE born during the horse-and-buggy days of 1875, moved out of the Dark Ages, so to speak, in 1930. That year, for the first time in the annals of the historic event, a stall machine was used to start the Derby and a public-address system was in operation at Churchill Downs.

The 1930 Derby's stall machine, known as the Waite device, replaced the old-fashioned web barrier starting method in which a net webbing was stretched across the track, then was sent up and away at the break by the starter. By today's starting-gate standards, the 1930 machine was rather crude. Still in its experimental stage, the machine was divided into stalls spread across the track and a tape was stretched in front. The horses lined up in the stalls, and, at the start, the tape was released. "The damn thing will never work," more than one skeptical horseman said of the starting machine, which just goes to show that trainers could be as wrong about innovations as they could be about horses.

As for the public-address system, one Derby Day newspaper story explained this new concept to its readers by stating, "Amplifiers from the stands will announce the progress of the race with the position of each leading horse and each horse coming up, quarter by quarter. As many of the packed-in mass will get to see little of the race, this feature will be the most popular of all the innovations."

On hand to call the Derby on radio were Graham McNamee and Clem McCarthy of NBC and Ted Husing of CBS. The announcers had a big job on their hands calling the Derby, a race that drew fifteen starters, headed by Gallant Fox.

Gallant Fox was ridden by Earl Sande, a veteran jockey making a comeback. Sande, who had won the 1923 Derby with Zev and the 1925 renewal aboard Flying Ebony, essentially had retired as a jockey in the late twenties to enter the business of owning and training a stable of horses, some of whom he occasionally rode. But he squandered his money on overpriced horses and was hurt by the stock-market crash. Given his financial situation, Sande was receptive to the idea of returning to active riding in 1930 and handling Gallant Fox for William Woodward, Sr., the owner of Belair Stud.

Gallant Fox won nine of ten races in 1930, each start with Sande aboard. The two were said to be "closer partners than Amos and Andy." Sande was known as the "Handy Guy," thanks to the poetry of Damon Runyon, and Gallant Fox was dubbed "The Fox of Belair."

That's not all that Gallant Fox was called. Some observers described the colt as downright lazy, one who wouldn't always put out his best effort. But Joe Pierce, a veteran horseman who exercised Gallant Fox, didn't exactly refer to the famous Thoroughbred as lazy—a loafer sometimes, but not lazy.

"Gallant Fox was a great, big, grand-looking horse and a big, *tough* horse," Pierce recalled years later. "He walked an hour in the morning before you'd put the saddle on him. And he'd work a mile and an eighth, a mile and a quarter. And in the afternoon he walked an hour, so he couldn't have been a lazy horse. He was just a tough horse."

Woodward once described Gallant Fox in similar fashion, saying, "He is really a rugged colt. He is not always a free-running colt, either. He will loaf a bit in his work and in his races."

Trainer "Sunny Jim" Fitzsimmons was known to use a relay team of horses to work out with Gallant Fox. One horse would start off with Gallant Fox, and, at some point along the way, another would step in and pick up the action, all the better to keep Gallant Fox running hard throughout the workout.

"He was a horse that if he got off by himself, he'd kinda loaf a little bit," said Pierce. "If he had a workhorse to go along with him, he'd put out a little more. But I wouldn't say he was a lazy horse. He just liked company."

He liked company in the afternoons as well as the mornings. A horse with a mind of his own, Gallant Fox didn't have what football coaches would call the "killer instinct." He never won a race by more than 4 lengths, and, all told, his eleven career triumphs were by a total of only 19½ lengths, which is less than Secretariat (31 lengths) and Count Fleet (25 or 30 lengths) in just *one* race, their Belmont Stakes victories of 1973 and 1943 respectively.

But what difference did it make that Gallant Fox didn't win overwhelmingly? He still got the job done more times than not, and Mr. Fitz, who trained an honor roll of champions through the years, paid Gallant Fox a supreme compliment by calling him the best horse he ever had going a mile and a half. Distance races indeed were right down Gallant Fox's alley. He twice won at a mile and a half and triumphed in three even longer races—a mile and five-eighths, a mile and three-quarters, and two miles.

Moreover, Gallant Fox's career earnings of $328,165 established a world record that lasted for a year, Sun Beau breaking it in 1931. In 1930, Gallant Fox also set a season's record of $308,275, a mark that stood until Assault's 1946 campaign.

Gallant Fox, a bay colt with a blazed face, was reported to be able to give his opponents an "evil eye." His right eye had an abundance of white around the pupil, and some racing people claimed that he would actually scare horses with a seemingly wild looking gaze.

Gallant Fox allegedly had something else going for him. In a day when testing wasn't done to detect drugs and horses frequently were hopped for races, Gallant Fox himself was said to have been "lighted up" on more than one occasion. But Pierce, the man who exercised Gallant Fox, dismissed this assertion.

"I wouldn't go along with that," Pierce said. "No sir, I would *not* go along with that. He was a good-feeling, tough horse, and a horse that took the training that he took, he didn't need any hop or anything like that. I wouldn't go along with that, and I was with him at all times and slept with him the night before the Derby. I slept right in his stall, in fact, so nothing could happen to him. I'd have to put that out the window, that remark. I'd have to say no, to my knowledge—unless somebody else knows something. I was with him almost all the time, and I'd have to say no."

Gallant Fox was foaled March 23, 1927 at Claiborne Farm, near Paris, Kentucky. He was sired by the imported Sir Gallahad III and was out of Marguerite. His dam produced three other fine runners—Petee-Wrack, who finished far back in the 1928 Derby; Fighting Fox, beaten favorite in the 1938 Derby; and Foxbrough. The latter two were full brothers of Gallant Fox.

Gallant Fox wasn't overly impressive as a two-year-old. Ridden by three different jockeys in 1929, the colt carved out a record of two victories, two seconds, and two thirds in seven starts. At three, he developed into a superstar.

With Sande aboard him for the first time, Gallant Fox triumphed by four lengths in the Wood Memorial and then scored by three-quarters of a length in the Preakness. Eight days later he ran in the Derby, going off as the 1.19-1 favorite. (Payoffs were to the penny during this period of Derby history.)

A crowd estimated from fifty to eighty thousand turned out for the Derby. Admission was $3, with an additional cost of $5.80 for the clubhouse. But not everybody paid. As was all too customary in those days, a large number of folks managed to gain admission to the track without paying those ticket prices.

As one news account reported:

> The stable grandstand, built to accommodate large numbers, failed to hold the race enthusiasts away from the grandstand. After getting into the stable inclosure by devious methods, the crowd, as usual, caught the guards looking away and rushed across to the grand-stand. A heavy wire fence topped with several strands of barbed wire offered no serious barrier.

The story added that "some enterprising boys, probably students of the Arabian Nights," offered a "magic carpet" ride for five cents.

> The system was for the visitor to seat himself on a strip of carpet and by means of boy power would find himself inside the formidable wire inclosure within a moment. The boys had dug the earth from under the fence and would pull the visitors, mostly women, through on the rug. Then, to complete the service, a boy stood inside ready to use a clothes brush. This, of course, cost another nickel.

It rained on Derby Day in 1930, the fourth straight year that umbrellas were needed by spectators attending this classic race. The condition of the track went from "fast" for the first four races on the card to "good" for the Derby.

The new starting machine was put in place at the top of the stretch for the Derby, an occurrence that didn't go unnoticed by at least one reporter who wrote, "Far up the track, half obscured by the rain, two draught horses dragged the row of dog-house stalls out on the track from which the horses were to start."

Then it was time for the horses to leave the paddock. "The parade to the post was to the strains of 'My Old Kentucky Home,' muted and slow and apparently with a soothing effect on the crowd, for there was little cheering until Gallant Fox and Sande came out seventh in line," reported *The New York Times*. "Then the cheers broke loose and Sande . . . lifted his cap."

Tannery came out later in the post parade, and, the paper noted, "the biggest yell was for him."

E. F. Prichard, the owner of Tannery, reportedly had wagered on this colt in the future book at odds as long as 100-1 and stood to pocket $200,000 in bets if his horse won the Derby. Future-book odds of 100-1 would seem to have been out of line on Tannery, who won five of eight races as a two-year-old and both of his starts at three—one by eight lengths, the other by one and a half—coming into the Derby.

On Derby Day, Tannery had enough supporters to go off as the 3.12-1 second choice in the betting.

Also lined up against Gallant Fox was 1929's best two-year-old filly, Alcibiades, who didn't particularly distinguish herself in her pre-Derby starts at three. Even though she was to go on and share acclaim with Snowflake as 1930's finest sophomore fillies, Alcibiades finished out of the money in her first three starts of the year before winning an allowance race three days before the Derby. Owned by Hal Price Headley, Alcibiades was among those grouped in the Derby's mutuel field.

For the most part, Gallant Fox's opposition was mediocre, at best, and the only way that he figured to lose the Derby was to get knocked down. Sande, of course, didn't intend for that to happen.

The fifteen entrants approached the stall machine, and the crowd, hushed in its anticipation of the start, heard the announcement over the amplifying system that the horses were at the post. The stall machine was new for this fifty-sixth Kentucky Derby and so was the public-address system, but the cry that rang out at the start was an old, familiar one—"They're off!"

With Gallant Fox starting from the number-seven post position, Sande quickly sensed trouble. These were rough-riding days, the era before the advent of the patrol film, and angling over from the number-twelve spot was Tannery, ridden by Willie Garner. Garner was attempting to shut off Gallant Fox, but Sande wasn't about to be outfoxed. Using his head, the cagey Sande gradually eased back with Gallant Fox and, to Garner's chagrin, eventually circled Tannery.

"I had dead aim on him at the start," Garner once recalled. "My intentions all the time was to come over and bother him 'cause I knew he was the horse to beat. So rather than him lettin' his horse break real fast, he just eased him back leavin' the gate 'cause he knew I was comin' over.

"He told me after the race, 'I knew you had dead aim on me.' Now a lot of riders like, if they wasn't too smart, they would have went ahead and broke fast and that would have given me time to come over and bother him, you see. I went on over, I bothered several others, but it didn't bother him. He pulled up leavin' the gate and then took around me. He was smart, the smartest you ever seen. He was always figurin' a quarter of a mile or three-eighths of a mile ahead of time."

Though in tight quarters the first time down the stretch, Sande soon moved Gallant Fox out into the clear and later into the lead. Gallant Fox led by 1½ or 2 lengths turning for home, and, after a mild midstretch bid by Gallant Knight proved fruitless, the message was coming through loud and clear. Gallant Fox was going to win, and he was going to make it look easy. He hit the finish line 2 lengths on top, Gallant Knight finishing second and Tannery eighth. Alcibiades, the early leader, faded to tenth. "Gallant Fox could have won by an even greater distance if he had been pressed, but there was no other horse in the race," wrote Grantland Rice.

By winning his third Derby, Sande tied the immortal nineteenth-century black jockey Isaac Murphy for the most victories in the classic. "Gallant Fox is a great colt," Sande

Earl Sande rode three Kentucky Derby winners—Zev (1923), Flying Ebony (1925), and Gallant Fox (1930). (Photo courtesy Keeneland-Cook)

said afterward. "He did everything I asked as willingly and as quickly today as any horse I have ever ridden."

Years later, in looking back on this victory by Gallant Fox, Sande said, "He probably would have won the Derby by ten lengths if I had let him run. But 'The Fox' was a temperamental horse, and you had to be careful how you rated him. If he got too far in front of the field he'd start to pull up, so in that 1930 Derby I kept him where he could hear the other horses back of him, and we didn't have any trouble."

Too bad "Sunny Jim" Fitzsimmons missed seeing it all. After saddling Gallant Fox for the Derby, Fitzsimmons went across the track to the infield to watch the race. "I was all ready to watch my horse do his stuff when I got caught in the crowd," Fitzsimmons later explained. "The next I knew was that the Belair Stud was on the receiving end of that party. I know it was a great race, even if I didn't see it."

It was customary during this stretch of Derby history for fans to flock onto the track after the race like so many geese. Of course, they had no business on the track, but Mr. Fitz certainly did. He wanted to walk onto the track to inspect Gallant Fox immediately afterward, but the strong arm of the law interfered.

"Pop didn't care for the crowd so he stayed in the infield," the trainer's son, John Fitzsimmons, recalled. "When the race was over, he tried to get across the track, and, of course, the track was full of people mobbing and milling around. Pop wanted to see the horse, see how he came back after the race, because it was a messy track. So he started to go across, and a mounted cop stopped him, swung his horse around, and nearly knocked Pop down. He said, 'You get out of there. Nobody allowed over in there except the trainers and owners.'"

One spectator who had a wonderful view of the proceedings was Lord Derby, for whose English family the Kentucky Derby and other derbies were named. He was a special guest at the 1930 Derby, watching the race from a pagoda specifically built for his visit. (It wasn't built in the infield, where the present structure stands, but was erected on the clubhouse side of the track.)

Afterward, in presenting the gold trophy to Woodward, Lord Derby said, "I came 5,000 miles to see this Derby. One's expectations are hardly ever realized; more rarely are they surpassed. In this case, I have had the unique experience of having enjoyed myself far in excess of my highest expectation. I was pleased to see a good horse win."

The mustachioed seventeenth earl of Derby, described as "a big, bluff-looking man," did mention during his stay in Kentucky that he would like to have an old-fashioned mint julep. To which one cynic cracked, "Yeah? Well, there are thousands of Kentuckians who are in the same fix."

Lord Derby also pointed out, to those who cared in the least, that as far as he was concerned, the correct pronunciation of the race was "darby," not "durby." To which the gifted Joe Palmer once addressed himself by writing that he'd bet that Americans didn't say "clark for clerk" because the English do. He added, "The Derby took out its naturalization papers somewhere in the '70s, and has since been advanced to full citizenship." Sorry about that, Lord Derby.

At any rate, Gallant Fox went on to capture the Belmont Stakes, the third leg in the Triple Crown.

The opponents that Gallant Fox defeated in the Derby weren't much. As a matter of fact, two of the worst horses in Derby history ran in the 1930 renewal—Dick O'Hara and Broadway Limited. Dick O'Hara dragged himself home in last place, which was where he finished in seven of fifteen career starts. Broadway Limited was a son of Man o' War, but "Big Red" would have disowned him. Broadway Limited failed to earn a penny in nine lifetime races.

Dick O'Hara and Broadway Limited weren't the 1930 Derby's only horses lacking in ability. Further underlining the overall weakness of Gallant Fox's opposition were these facts:

• With the exception of Gallant Knight, who earned $134,229, not a single other opponent brought home as much as $50,000 in career purse money.

• Gallant Fox's lifetime earnings fell only $25,454 short of matching the entire career productions of *all* fourteen other starters. Gallant Fox earned his $328,165 in 17 starts, an average of $19,304 per race. The other fourteen earned $353,619 in 693 starts, averaging all of $510 per outing.

• Five of the 1930 Derby starters, or one-third the field, never won a race after running for the roses. Two of them, Crack Brigade and Kilkerry, didn't even start again. The unsound Kilkerry, injured during a workout leading up to the Derby, came out of the race lame. Crack Brigade also showed signs of lameness the day after the Derby, though it reportedly wasn't considered serious.

• Uncle Luther, who injured his right foreleg slightly in the Derby, went 0 for 6 the rest of his career, Dick O'Hara 0 for 4, and Broadway Limited 0 for 2. Broadway Limited and Uncle Luther died less than four months after the Derby, the former succumbing to heart failure in an August 29 race and the latter killed September 7 in a training accident.

Most of the 1930 Derby starters were never to make headlines after their three-year-old seasons, but two of them at least deserved to be called "iron horses." The appropriately named Longus had a long, long career, extending through 1938. His record showed 222 starts, 31 victories, 26 seconds, and 30 thirds. Ned O., third in the Derby, finished his career with 27 victories, 25 seconds, and 19 thirds from 155 starts.

As for Gallant Fox, he was retired after his 1930 campaign. In his first two seasons at stud, he sired 1935 Triple Crown champion Omaha and Granville, who was acclaimed Horse of the Year in 1936.

Gallant Fox, the only Triple Crown champion ever to sire a Triple Crown winner, accomplished relatively little at stud after those impressive first two crops. At the age of twenty-seven, the old horse died early in the afternoon on November 13, 1954, the same day that the Gallant Fox Handicap was run at Jamaica and the Marguerite Stakes, a race named for his dam, was run at Pimlico.

"I'm sure sorry to hear about the 'Old Fox' passing away," said Sande. "He was a great pal, and at running a distance he was terrific—one of the best horses I ever rode."

His remains were buried at Claiborne Farm, his birth-place. Gallant Fox (1927-54) was one of the immortals.

12

A "Savage" Racehorse
by the Name of Omaha

PLAIN OLD-FASHIONED HORSE SENSE tells you it's not a wise policy to smart off to the boss, whoever he or she might be. More than one person has wound up in an unemployment line after having opened his mouth and unleashed some vitriolic comments to the person paying his salary. But in the case of jockey Willie ("Smokey") Saunders, saying the wrong thing to his boss once turned out to be a blessing in disguise. Fact is, it led to his riding the famous racehorse Omaha to victory in the 1935 Triple Crown.

First we need some background. Unlike today, riding goggles weren't in vogue years ago. So with clods of soil flying and sand spraying through the air, jockeys were apt to get dirt in their eyes.

After finishing next to last aboard the Wheatley Stable's Carry Over in the 1934 Wood Memorial, Saunders was having trouble seeing, his eyes irritated with sand from the old Jamaica racetrack in New York. "This coarse sand was cutting my eyes," Saunders recalled. "I couldn't even blink my eyes. And I was following my valet back to the jocks' room. In fact, I had ahold of his sleeve, lettin' him more or less lead me back so I wouldn't cut my eyeballs with the sand.

"This woman walked up to me and she said in an English accent, 'What happened to my hawss?' I couldn't see very well due to the sand in my eyes. All I can do is look down, and I look down, there's a woman standing there with cotton

Omaha, with Willie ("Smokey") Saunders up. (Photo courtesy Keeneland-Cook)

hose and half-soled shoes. I figured it was some two-dollar-show bettor.

"And I said, 'Lady, why don't you go home and cook your husband's meals and quit losin' his hard-earned money on these bad horses.' And I went into the jocks' room."

Unbeknownst to Saunders, the lady was Mrs. Henry Carnegie Phipps, who owned the Wheatley Stable with her brother, Ogden Mills.

Saunders, who had never met Mrs. Phipps, was in for a surprise the next morning when he went to the barn of "Sunny Jim" Fitzsimmons, trainer for the Wheatley Stable and Belair Stud.

"Gee, I have to let you go," Mr. Fitz told him.

"What do you mean?" Saunders replied.

Mr. Fitz then told him that the lady he was talking to at the track the previous day happened to be none other than the Boss Lady. "Well, don't worry about it," he told Saunders. "I'll have to put you with Belair Stud. You can't ride for her anymore as long as she's here."

But that didn't mean Saunders never rode again for Mrs. Phipps. "I could ride for her when she was out of the country," he said with a chuckle. "When she couldn't get the results, see."

The bottom line on this chain of events was that Saunders wound up riding Omaha. "Just shows you how fate is," Saunders said. "Saying the wrong thing at the right time helped me win the Triple Crown, actually."

Saunders, who began riding Omaha in his three-year-old season in 1935, recalled that the colt would "savage" another horse that would bump or brush him. That is, Omaha would try to take a bite out of a horse that made contact with him. Saunders learned about this habit during a workout.

"They used to work two horses with him," Saunders said. "They'd work a horse the first half-mile, and then they'd hook another horse in with him, and they broke this horse off the outside fence to hook in with him. He [an exercise rider] didn't get his horse straightened out quick enough and brushed me when he come in. When he did, why, he [Omaha] got ahold of him right now.

"So I immediately got to the exercise boy, and I said, 'Ooohhh, whatever you do, don't ever tell anybody.' Because all someone would have had to do was run some bum in there as an entry mate—'cause I come from way back— lay back there, and when I started to move, move out and bump me. And he would have stopped and went to fighting instead of running. Naturally, I was very cautious. That's one reason that I always had to take him around horses, rather than take a chance on a horse hitting him."

Saunders said it was a well-kept secret, Omaha's desire to bite into any horse that would bump him. "Other than the exercise boy, myself, and Mr. Fitzsimmons, I think we were the only ones that knew about it," Saunders said. "Thank God, nobody else knew it."

Omaha was foaled at Claiborne Farm on March 24, 1932. A golden chestnut with a prominent blaze, he was a son of Gallant Fox, who is the only Triple Crown champion ever to sire a winner of these three coveted races—the Kentucky Derby, Preakness, and Belmont. Omaha developed into a big, long-bodied colt who was to stand 16 hands, 2½ inches during the prime of his racing career. He took up more space than one of those modern-day University of Nebraska offensive linemen. To be sure, Omaha was so large that he required double-room accommodations at the racetrack. "Everywhere we went with him, why, they'd have to give him two stalls," Saunders said. "They'd take two stalls and knock the partition out in the middle and make one huge stall of it."

Omaha was bred and owned by William Woodward, Sr., one of the most influential figures in the history of American racing. Woodward, a New York banker who owned Belair Stud in Maryland, described himself as a Victorian. He traditionally spoke, dressed, and carried himself with the greatest of dignity, conservatism, and authority. Woodward bred more than ninety stakes winners in the United States and Europe. In Omaha, he bred a colt who proved to be a classic distance performer, a long-winded runner who had the stamina that is found lacking in so many horses these days.

Omaha didn't demonstrate as a two-year-old that greatness was awaiting him on the racetrack. In the first start of his career, he finished second, a nose behind Sir Lamorak. Omaha bore in on the winner in that race, and in his next start he came in on the leading Allen Z. in the stretch before veering out nearing the finish. Only this time, Omaha managed to win, scoring a head victory. It was to be his only triumph in nine races as a two-year-old, though he did finish second in three stakes—the Sanford, Champagne, and Junior Champion.

Omaha won his first start as a three-year-old before finishing a fast-closing third in the Wood Memorial. Both races were at a mile and seventy yards. He then was sent to Louisville to run for the roses.

A crowd of 53,031 turned out in dreary weather for the Derby. The gathering included millionaires and derelicts, horsemen and hookers, Southern belles and platinum blondes, politicians and Kentucky colonels. For the most part their ardor was dampened by a drizzling rain that fell during the afternoon, sending umbrellas springing upward like mushrooms in the Churchill Downs' grassy infield.

The New York Times reported:

> Racegoers were surprised upon arrival at the track to see the famous old plant with many of the earmarks of an armed camp. Heavy wire barriers had been erected on the inside rail between various sections of the grand stand and at strategic points on the backstretch. In addition, soldiers appeared to be everywhere.
>
> This was due to the assignment of several hundred

men from the National Guard. They were stationed all
the way along both rails up and down the homestretch.
The infield crowd was kept rather definitely under
control by the adroit use of clubs as this or that group
became obstreperous.

The 1935 Derby marked the first time that the National
Guard was on duty at the race. In years past, the Louisville
police couldn't keep the crowd under control. For example,
many fans traditionally would race across the track from the
infield right before the Derby and muscle their way into the
clubhouse box seats. The Louisville police said they were
helpless against these determined youths.

The National Guard wasn't helpless, though, and, arriving on the scene in 1935, it literally swung big sticks, some
Guardsmen actually carrying baseball bats.

In spite of the presence of armed guards, a battery of
boys did rush a clubhouse door and hurtled inside, each
darting into a different direction and thus defying pursuit.

These youths weren't the only ones who approached a
gate without a ticket. Philadelphia sportsman J. H.
Louchheim, owner of Derby starter Morpluck, wagered
$1,000 shortly before the race on his horse, who was des-
tined to finish no better than seventh. After making the bet,
Louchheim forged his way through the milling crowd to
reach his box. He was stopped at the gate and asked for his
return ticket stub. He couldn't find it. That's not all he
couldn't find. After a search, he discovered that the mutuel
tickets he had just purchased on Morpluck were missing.

Welcome to the Derby, Mr. Louchheim.

With early future-book favorite Chance Sun going wrong
and being withdrawn from the Derby just days before the
classic, Calumet Farm's Nellie Flag, a filly, was sent off as a
moderate favorite in a race that was considered wide open.
Nellie Flag had a blue-blooded racing heritage. Her mother,
Nellie Morse, succeeded in whipping fourteen males in winning the 1924 Preakness, and her grandfather was none
other than the immortal Man o' War. Nellie Flag was the

second of many stakes winners to represent the Calumet Farm of Warren Wright, Sr., and she was the first horse ever to run in the Kentucky Derby for the Lexington Thoroughbred nursery. She also was the first horse ever ridden in the classic by a long-nosed, nineteen-year-old jockey by the name of Eddie Arcaro, who was to go on to win five Derbies in his distinguished career.

The Derby was a rough race for both Nellie Flag, who was bumped hard two or three times en route to her fourth-place finish, and for a certain infield spectator, who was booted one good time. "Someone was sitting on the inside rail with their feet over it, and one horse hit him and knocked him back in the center field," Saunders recalled. "Fortunately, nothing happened. No horse got hurt, rider or spectator or anything."

Omaha enjoyed smooth sailing in the Derby, as longtime Louisville newspaperman Mike Barry recalled. Barry would never forget the sight of jockey Lester Balaski whipping a tattoo on Roman Soldier's behind in a bid to overtake Omaha coming down the homestretch. But Balaski's efforts were in vain, Omaha hitting the finish line a length and a half ahead of Roman Soldier.

Barry remembered more than just the race. It seems a man had approached him a month before the Derby with a future-book bet of $10 to win on Omaha, whose odds were 5-1 at the time. Barry got together with a friend, Bud Snider, and said, 'Bud, I'll split the bet with you. It's a month before the Derby. If he doesn't start, we win the guy's $10. And if he does start, we can always bet it.'"

So Barry and Snider held the $10 and played a waiting game. If Omaha made it to the Derby, then they would bet the $10 on him at the track. He did, but they didn't.

With Omaha starting from the number-ten post position in the big field of eighteen, Barry got a bright idea. "This big, awkward mule will never get out of that crowd," Barry told Snider. "We'll just hold the bet."

Barry watched the race from a spot on the clubhouse

turn. He couldn't believe his eyes when the race unfolded as it did. "Everybody inside of him goes to the inside, everybody outside of him goes to the outside, and here he is just like they had cleared the track for him," Barry recalled. "He comes by me, he's about fifth, and Saunders looks like a guy sitting up there on top of a Cadillac running against Volkswagens. This big, long-striding colt was absolutely clear, and there was no question about the outcome of the race."

If Barry and Snider had bet the $10 on Omaha at the mutuel windows that day, they would have collected on 4-1 odds and thus would have had to come across with $10 out of their own pockets to make up the difference on the 5-1 future-book wager that they had taken. But by holding the bet, they had to cough up $25 each. "And $25 apiece in 1935 was a *fortune*," Barry said.

It was a costly lesson, but in time it paid rich dividends for Snider. "That's been forty years ago," Barry recalled in the 1970s, "and he hasn't listened to me on a horse since."

Barry and Snider weren't the only ones licking their wounds after the Omaha Derby. So were bookies in Omaha. The Associated Press reported from Omaha in a dispatch on Derby Day:

> Sentiment paid dividends as high as 4 to 1 in Omaha today. When the horse Omaha went to the starting post at Louisville, Omahans for sentimental reasons went to the bookmakers. Many who never played a race in their lives bet a few dollars by way of showing their appreciation to William Woodward, Omaha's owner. Local bookmakers, unmoved by the wave of civic pride, covered the bets themselves. They glumly admitted tonight they took a lacing for sums estimated by some to total $80,000.

Excitement over the 1935 Derby continued in Omaha. "Flash from Omaha! This time meaning a city in Nebraska," Buck Weaver wrote in *The Louisville Times* shortly after the race. "They're willing to put on a 'special,' with plenty of dough attendant, some folk who operate a track called Ak-Sar-Ben, to induce a horse named Omaha back to the city of his 'nativity.' One must admire their spirit, but their chances of gaining an audience from the Derby winner are exceedingly slim. Too many more swellegant affairs in the more populous centers in sight." Weaver, who said Omaha was "the orneriest looking hide" in the Derby, was right about Ak-Sar-Ben's chances of luring the colt. Omaha was never to race at Ak-Sar-Ben, but the colt's admirers in Nebraska still took a great interest in his career.

Meanwhile, back in Kentucky, Omaha's name had aroused the curiosity of many, and Bruce Dudley, sports editor of *The Courier-Journal* in Louisville, set out to explain it in his account of the Derby.

> The question, "Why was the horse named Omaha?" was asked many hundreds of times Saturday. When Omaha was a yearling, Mr. Woodward showed him to some friends who commented on his "beefiness" and Mr. Woodward decided to name him for some beef-packaging center. He couldn't call him "Chicago," for a horse recently had been named that, and "Kansas City" didn't especially strike him, so he called him Omaha.

Following the 1935 Triple Crown, *The New York Times* reported, "Mr. Woodward desired a name beginning with 'O' to carry out the suggestion found in the blood lines of such horses in the male descent as Bend Or, Ormonde and Orme. After thinking it over, he hit upon the name of the Nebraska city."

The crowd that gathered for the 1935 Derby got into the mood of things in pure Kentucky style. As Richard S. Davis wrote in *The Milwaukee Journal*, it was not a day for a horse race.

> Missing and lamented were the typical Derby costumes of the flower and beauty of the South. Heavy

coats, slickers and sweaters were the proper costume
for the day and pictorially the crowd was dismally
drab, but there was recompense—ah, yes, warm recompense. Kentucky, as you know, is famous for other
products than rapid horses, and one of these is the
juice of the corn. It is betraying no confidence to report that this was a day for the bottle and from the
bottle came gaiety.

On the presentation stand after the Derby, Kentucky governor Ruby Laffoon presented the gold trophy to
Woodward, who said in his deep voice over the radio, "I
have the intense pleasure of winning the Kentucky Derby
with the son of my great horse, Gallant Fox."

Another dignitary on the award platform was Postmaster
General James A. Farley, whose presence prompted
Woodward to talk politics. "This is not a new deal,"
Woodward was quoted as saying. "This is an old deal. And it
is a good solid deal—because Thoroughbred bloodlines
bring out champions when properly crossed."

That's not all Woodward said. He had had a drink or two
(or three or four) that day, and, as a result, he couldn't re-
strain himself on the radio airwaves.

"That was sort of funny," Saunders recalled. "Whoever
doing the interviewing was trying to interview Farley and
Mr. Woodward and me. And Mr. Woodward kept saying,
'Jim, you're a fine fellow, but that Roosevelt, he is no good.'
They'd have to shut us off, and then they'd start interviewing him again, and he'd get back into that same little deal
and we'd get cut off again."

The inevitable comparison of Omaha with his father,
Gallant Fox, was a subject of conversation after the Derby.
"The Fox, nobody will ever know just how good he really
was," said the white-mustached Woodward, looking distinguished in a Homburg hat and brown suit. "But his son is
like him—a really good horse. The Fox showed us how
good he was. Omaha still has to do that."

From the Derby, Omaha scored an overwhelming victory in the Preakness. By six lengths, he came coasting home on top before forty to forty-five thousand fans at Pimlico. His time of 1:58⅖ on a fast racing strip was a mere two-fifths of a second slower than the track record.

In his next race, Omaha was sent off as a 1-2 favorite in the Withers Mile but came back a 1½-length loser to Rosemont.

For a while, Omaha looked like a loser again in his try for the Triple Crown at Belmont. "He was not a real good 'off-track' horse, being so large," Saunders said. "The Belmont was run in deep mud, which was the hardest race on him. He just did win that. At one time, I thought he might get beat. At about the half-mile pole, I didn't think he was going to make it. He couldn't get ahold of the racetrack, but he finally got it together and went on and got it."

Readers of *The New York Times* came across the following account of the Belmont from Bryan Field, one of the most knowledgeable men ever to write about racing:

> Slashing onward through a drenching rain and slippery footing, Omaha yesterday won the historic Belmont Stakes before 25,000 persons in a manner definitely to establish himself as the champion 3-year-old of 1935. . . . Omaha was a 7-to-10 shot with the big Belmont Park crowd which braved one of the wettest, rawest days of the year. . . . Saunders waited so long and he waited so well that some thought Omaha beaten at the top of the stretch. But at the finish the only horse forging on with any show of strength and power was the winner.

Following his Triple Crown sweep, the "Belair Bullet" raced two weeks later against older horses in the Brooklyn Handicap. Omaha finished a badly beaten third behind the victorious Discovery, who set a world record for the mile and one-eighth.

Omaha returned to the three-year-old division and won

the Dwyer impressively. Then came the Arlington Classic, a 1¼-mile race that Omaha captured in a track-record time of 2:01⅖. It was on to Saratoga for Omaha, but unfortunately he went lame temporarily and didn't race the rest of the year.

Woodward, who also raced a stable in England, had an ambition for years to win the historic Ascot Gold Cup, and, in Omaha, he thought he had a horse capable of doing it. After Capt. Cecil Boyd-Rochfort, Woodward's English trainer, inspected Omaha in New York, the word was "go" for England.

Omaha left New York on January 8, 1936, aboard the liner *Aquitania*. He occupied a *C*-deck stall that had been well padded to guard against accident in the event of rough seas. One week later, Omaha arrived in England, attendants saying he stood the ocean trip very well.

Omaha's first start in England came on May 9 in the 1½-mile Victor Wild Stakes at Kempton Park. Whereas Omaha had been accustomed to running in a counterclockwise direction at American tracks, races at Kempton were run in a clockwise direction, which was considered excellent preparation for Ascot, also a clockwise track. Many fans in the big crowd at Kempton, skeptical of Omaha, wagered their shillings on Montrose. But just before the start, the smart money was bet in large amounts on Omaha, who was sent off as the favorite and who didn't let his bettors down. Passing his opponents at the head of the stretch as though they were standing still, he scored a 1½-length victory, carrying 129 pounds.

"Omaha is one of the greatest horses I've ever ridden," said Pat Beasley, the chap who rode the colt. "He was full of run all the way, but I held him back until we rounded the last bend. All I had to do was turn him loose."

In his next start, on May 30, many British bookmakers refused to take bets on Omaha at any odds, bringing derisive comments, especially from Americans who had flocked to Kempton Park to watch the colt in the two-mile Queen's

Plate. Omaha, going off as the 10-11 favorite and carrying 130 pounds, came from last place and defeated Lord Derby's Bobsleigh by a neck in a desperately exciting stretch duel.

And then on June 18, it was time for the race Woodward so wanted to win—the Ascot Gold Cup. Omaha gave one of the finest efforts of his career in this race, albeit a losing one. In a stirring battle, he and Quashed, a four-year-old filly owned by Lord Stanley, hooked up about a half-mile from the finish at the bottom of the uphill stretch, and they ran together in a head-and-head duel that had the crowd of 150,000 at Ascot cheering wildly.

At the end of the 2½-mile test, it was Quashed the winner over the favored Omaha—but only by inches. "The defeat added more to the stature of Omaha than his Triple Crown victories in the United States," Kent Hollingsworth wrote in the book *The Great Ones.*

Trainer Boyd-Rochfort cited three reasons for Omaha's defeat. The colt had come over to England two months later than was ideal. For the first time in his career, he had become extremely upset before a race. And his British jockey had suffered the misfortune of having his whip knocked from his hand by Quashed's rider about one hundred yards from the finish.

A fortnight later, Omaha was sent to the post again, this time carrying 138 pounds in the 1½-mile Princess of Wales' Stakes at Newmarket. Once again, he became upset before the race. He sweated so heavily in the paddock that one writer claimed the colt must have lost 7 pounds before he went to the course. Simply not on his best behavior that day, Omaha refused to face the gate, delaying the start six minutes. Finally the race was under way, and, at the end, after he had done all that sweating and then acted up at the start, Omaha finished second on a rain-soaked course, losing by a neck to Taj Akbar, the 1936 Epsom Derby runner-up owned by the Aga Khan.

Taj Akbar received eighteen pounds from Omaha.

"British turf writers agreed the load packed on the American champion blighted his hopes before he left the paddock," the Associated Press reported. "Several declared, 'He's greater than either Reigh Count or Twenty Grand [two previous Kentucky Derby winners who also had raced in England], but no horse in the world could win with such a handicap.'"

The Princess of Wales' Stakes turned out to be the last race of Omaha's career. Though he was kept in England to compete in the 1937 Ascot Gold Cup, he went lame before the race and subsequently was returned to the United States. He was retired to stud and sent to Claiborne Farm, where he had been born.

Sadly, Omaha was a failure as a stallion. In time he was leased to The Jockey Club's Lookout Stallion Station, in Avon, New York, before heading out in 1950 to Nebraska, where he spent his final years at Grove Porter's farm in Nebraska City. Porter's son, Morton, accompanied Omaha on his train trip to Nebraska from New York.

"It was a great trip for me," Morton Porter once told *Daily Racing Form* columnist Barney Nagler. "He wasn't crated, mind you, like an ordinary horse might have been but stood loose in the car. Everywhere we went, when we stopped, I would roll back the door and people would come up to the car and look at Omaha. They didn't know him, but they asked who he was and I'd tell them and they'd be impressed. It took us two and one-half days.

"We brought him out to the races here at Ak-Sar-Ben. He was low in the back and we wondered how he would handle himself. Well, we put him in the old winner's circle, which was sandy, and when the bell went off for the start of a race, wouldn't you know it, he almost jumped the rail to get into the thing."

Omaha, the old warrior, passed away in 1959 and was buried at Ak-Sar-Ben Racetrack in a grave marked by a monument erected in his honor.

13

Paul Jones Finally Gained Respect in the Derby

SPECTACULAR BID, WHO REPRESENTED Baltimore's Meyerhoff family so brilliantly by winning the Kentucky Derby, Preakness, and other major races, has enjoyed a life of leisure and love in retirement. Another Kentucky Derby winner with Baltimore connections never had it quite so good. Paul Jones, who won the 1920 Kentucky Derby for Baltimore's Ral Parr, didn't have any romantic involvement

Ral Parr, co-owner of 1920 Kentucky Derby winner Paul Jones. (Photo courtesy Keeneland-Cook)

after his racing days ended. Paul Jones, you see, was a gelding and spent his retirement days as a qualified hunter in
Virginia.

Spectacular Bid was all racehorse and all "man," but Paul
Jones could have been excused if he suffered from the
Rodney Dangerfield complex. He didn't get much respect.

Where Spectacular Bid won the 1979 Kentucky Derby as
an odds-on favorite, Paul Jones captured the 1920 renewal
at a 16-1 price. Moreover, he generally wasn't even rated the
better half of a two-horse entry that ran in the Derby. He
was considered a second stringer to Blazes, his stablemate
who finished sixth. After the Derby, Paul Jones was described by one newspaper as "despised and ignored, the
'weak sister' of his stable." Another publication referred to
him as "the ugly little brown."

Shortly before the Derby, another account referred to
Paul Jones as a colt, a mistake that other publications sometimes made, and said he wasn't an impressive-looking horse.
"No upstanding, commanding horse is he; rather a sedate
and workmanlike sort, but horses do not run on looks and
looks are chiefly a sales ring asset," the story said. A Bo
Derek of racehorses, he obviously wasn't.

Spectacular Bid earned his niche in racing history as one
of the sport's all-time greats, but Paul Jones was a horse who
was never truly great, sometimes good, and usually a loser.
Spectacular Bid, who sold for $37,000 as a yearling, won
twenty-six of thirty races and earned $2,781,607, then a
world record. On top of that, he was syndicated for stud duty at a price of $22 million, also a record at that time. Back
in 1918, Paul Jones sold for $1,000 as a yearling. He went on
to win only fourteen of sixty-five races and earn $64,171 in
purses.

Moreover, Spectacular Bid broke seven track records and
equaled another. Paul Jones set one track record (a shallow
one, at that).

In all fairness to Paul Jones, virtually all horses would
come up short in comparison to Spectacular Bid. But even

so, the bottom line on Paul Jones was that he was only a solid performer, at best. Oh, if things went right for Paul Jones, if he caught the right kind of track and/or if the weights were in his favor, he might be worth a bet. Otherwise, he was usually best forgotten.

Paul Jones' two most important victories came on "off" tracks, the Kentucky Derby and Suburban Handicap. Although 64.6 percent of his starts (forty-two of sixty-five) were on fast tracks, only 35.7 percent of his triumphs (five of fourteen) were on fast strips. Three victories were on slow tracks, two each in muddy and sloppy going, and one each on a heavy and good track.

He lost to Man o' War twice, by a total of at least 26¾ lengths. Succumbing to Man o' War was no disgrace, but he was no threat to the fabled horse's younger brother either, My Play. Paul Jones was fifth in both meetings with My Play, losing by a total of 16 lengths.

Paul Jones and Exterminator, the 1918 Kentucky Derby winner, were longtime rivals, facing each other in ten races from 1920 to 1923. In every race, Exterminator carried much more weight than Paul Jones—an average difference of better than nineteen pounds per meeting. Exterminator finished ahead of Paul Jones in all but three of their ten meetings.

Paul Jones was bred in Kentucky by John E. Madden, the "Wizard of the Turf," and was bought on Parr's behalf by trainer William ("Uncle Billy") Garth at the Saratoga yearling sale. Following his purchase, the Parr stable decided to geld Paul Jones in the hope of changing his mean temper. Gelding him "brought a wonderful change in his habits," it was reported after the Derby, "but he is still none too gentle a thoroughbred."

Ownership of a racehorse isn't always as clear as it might appear on paper. In the case of Paul Jones, he carried Parr's colors—black and white stripes and red sash—for the first two years of his career (1919-20) and wound up running in J. S. Cosden's name for his final two seasons (1922-23) and

John E. Madden, the "Wizard of the Turf," bred 1920 Kentucky Derby winner Paul Jones. (Photo courtesy Keeneland Library)

all but one race in 1921. According to *Daily Racing Form* charts, Paul Jones raced in Parr's name twenty-six times, Cosden's thirty-nine.

It was reported at the time of the 1920 Kentucky Derby that Cosden was involved with Parr in the ownership of the gelding. Another story referred to Garth as the trainer of the "Parr-Cosden stable." Adding a different twist to the ownership of Paul Jones was a 1930 story stating that he actually was owned by Garth, the trainer, at the time of the Derby. In all likelihood, Paul Jones was owned in partnership by Parr and Cosden throughout his racing days.

Maryland was a familiar battleground for Paul Jones. Thirty-nine of his sixty-five starts were in the Old Line State—fifteen at the old Havre de Grace track, ten each at Laurel Park and Pimlico, and four at Bowie. Additionally, he had twenty-one starts in New York, four in Illinois, and one in Kentucky.

Paul Jones, by Sea King—May Florence, was brought out for his unveiling early in his two-year-old season at Bowie. On April 7, 1919, he finished second in a maiden race, beaten half a length by Calvert, an odds-on favorite. Next, at Havre de Grace, Paul Jones found himself running in another maiden race, except this one was a maiden claiming race, meaning that this horse who was to go on and win the Kentucky Derby could have been claimed—or purchased— in the second start of his career. To Parr's good fortune, Paul Jones wasn't claimed. The horse didn't win either, finishing third on a sloppy track to Peter Combs, a two-year-old owned by the Glen Riddle Farm and trained by Louis Feustel. Glen Riddle and Feustel had another two-year-old who had not yet started, a horse against whom Paul Jones would later run. His name was Man o' War.

Where the third and fourth races of Spectacular Bid's career resulted in his first two defeats, starts three and four produced the first two victories for Paul Jones.

In his third start, the Aberdeen Stakes at Havre de Grace, Paul Jones triumphed by a nose on a heavy track and paid

$31.80 on a $2-win bet. Paul Jones, who earned $892.21, carried 109 pounds, the lightest weight in the field of five.

Paul Jones didn't go off as a long shot in his next outing. He was the 4-5 favorite, and he won as a 4-5 favorite should. By four lengths he came romping home on top at Pimlico, this time packing high weight of 117 pounds.

After those four races in Maryland, Paul Jones was sent off to New York, where he would meet up with a better group of two-year-olds. On May 30, 1919, he ran in a five-furlong allowance race that drew Dominique, who was owned by Madden, the breeder of Paul Jones. Dominique, a strong favorite, made it look easy in winning by six lengths. Paul Jones ran second.

Paul Jones hadn't had a meaningful relationship with any of his jockeys in his first five races—four different men had ridden him—but in his sixth start he was introduced to Ted Rice, and they hit it off well from the start. Just four days after he had lost to Dominique, Paul Jones came back with Rice riding him competitively for the first time and won the Bouquet Selling Stakes at Belmont Park. Going off as the odds-on favorite and carrying top weight of 112 pounds, Paul Jones seized the early lead and stayed in front all the way to triumph by a length. The track was fast, but Paul Jones' time for the five furlongs wasn't. His :59²/₅ clocking fell a full 3⁴/₅ seconds off the Belmont record.

Dominique wasn't in that race, but he and Paul Jones crossed paths again six days later in a five-furlong allowance at Belmont. This time Dominique raced for horseman Sam Hildreth instead of Madden. In their first meeting ten days earlier the track was fast, but it was slow for this race and Paul Jones got the job done. He won by a length over Dominique, the overwhelming favorite who "apparently was running easily, but tired and sprawled in the final sixteenth," according to *Daily Racing Form*'s chart. Rice was aboard Paul Jones for this second straight victory.

Paul Jones moved on to Saratoga, finishing fourth in the Flash Stakes and third in the Albany Handicap. He didn't compete in the Sanford Memorial on August 13, 1919, the only race that Man o' War ever lost, but a month later—on September 13—Paul Jones met "Big Red" in the Futurity Stakes at Belmont Park. Paul Jones tired in the stretch and wound up sixth or seventh, beaten at least 8¼ lengths by Man o' War.

A week later, Paul Jones came in fourth in the Eastern Shore Stakes at Havre de Grace. He started one more time as a juvenile, scoring a head victory in a mile allowance at Havre de Grace. His time of 1:41 set a track record. The record, however, wasn't all that significant because it was only the second time a mile race had been run at the Maryland track.

Paul Jones' two-year-old record was decent, but not spectacular—five victories, two seconds, and two thirds in twelve starts with earnings of $6,404. Paul Jones, who wintered in Maryland, had promise, but nobody could seriously think that he would win the 1920 Kentucky Derby.

Paul Jones and Blazes were among 107 nominees to the Derby. Paul Jones was listed in *The Thoroughbred Record* magazine's listing of Derby candidates as a colt, an error that even popped up in the Churchill Downs program on Derby Day.

The '20 Derby would wind up pulling together plenty of horses, but not *the* horse. Man o' War wasn't among those nominated to the Kentucky Derby. The *Daily Racing Form*'s knowledgeable C. C. Ridley, in handicapping the three-year-olds leading up to the 1920 season, ranked Blazes second on the list at 120 pounds. Man o' War was a runaway first at 136.

At the start of their three-year-old seasons, Paul Jones and Blazes each had two pre-Derby races at Havre de Grace. On April 17, Blazes won a six-furlong sprint. Four days later, Paul Jones did the same. They met on April 24 in the mile-and-seventy-yard Chesapeake Stakes. Paul Jones came in second, Blazes fourth.

Then it was on to Kentucky. Blazes, a colt, and Paul Jones arrived at Churchill Downs on April 29, nine days before the Derby. Parr came to Louisville along with the horses.

The Louisville Times noted that Paul Jones and Blazes shipped well and "looked fit as a fiddle" when they were taken out on the track.

Unlike today, old-time trainers weren't reluctant to work their Derby candidates the distance of the race, a mile and a quarter. Just three days before the 1920 Derby, at least nine eventual starters—or more than half the field of seventeen—worked that distance. Of the nine, Bersagliere had the fastest time (2:06), By Golly the slowest (2:10⅘).

The Parr twosome each went a mile and a quarter that day, working together, and their time was just slightly faster than By Golly's. "Paul Jones led his companion home," reported *The Courier-Journal.* "Both were pushed at the end of a mile and a quarter in 2:10⅖. Blazes apparently was a tired horse after the trial."

Garth started off the year with high Derby hopes for Blazes. A month before the big race, *The Thoroughbred Record* magazine reported:

> William Garth, who is training the Parr-Cosden stable again this year, recently declared in the East that he was ready to back Blazes at even money, play or pay, against any three-year-old entered in the Kentucky Derby. The long-legged, short-bodied son of Wrack-Blazing Star was more than a good two-year-old last year, but he had a pretty stiff campaign. He is said to have wintered unusually well and to be as lusty as a bear.

On Derby Day, though, *The Louisville Herald* stated that Garth liked Paul Jones' chances better than he did Blazes'. "Paul Jones and Blazes have outside chances, especially if the track is muddy," the paper said. "The first named has been working better than Blazes, and is better fancied by trainer Billy Garth, who says both colts [*sic*] are fit and ready to run."

Experts didn't particularly like either horse's chances. Blazes wasn't picked to finish in the money in any of the

seven Derby selections (five publications and two individu-
als) that appeared in *The Louisville Times* on Derby Day. Paul
Jones was mentioned in one of those selections. *The
Louisville Times* tabbed him to finish third.

A person could have been confused by reading this newspaper leading up to the Derby. On Monday of Derby Week,
Robert E. Dundon observed, "The writer is of the opinion
that the best showing in actual racing, all conditions taken
into their true perspective, made this spring, is by Paul
Jones, one of the two star colts [*sic*] which will be sent to the
post by Ral Parr of Maryland. He also holds to the belief

*Ral Parr (left), co-owner of Paul Jones, with J. S. Cosden (center) and
Harry Payne Whitney in 1917.* (Photo courtesy Keeneland-Cook)

that Upset has shown the best actual form for the Whitney stable, and that it is a close thing between Blazes and Peace Pennant for third, on their form to date." Here Dundon had correctly picked the Derby one-two, but he proceeded to change his mind and didn't go with Paul Jones on the day of the race.

Two days before the Derby, Verney ("Screw") Sanders, another writer for *The Louisville Times,* told his readers, "Should the track be heavy, Blazes will be hard to beat. I believe he is better than Paul Jones, though his stable companion was second to Sandy Beal in the Chesapeake Stakes, and Blazes finished fourth in that event."

Twenty-two horses were entered in the Derby, including five couplings. Five were scratched, leaving four entries and seventeen starters that ranked at the time as the largest in Derby history. The Harry Payne Whitney three-horse entry of Damask, Wildair, and Upset was favored, and the G. W. Loft coupling of Donnacona and On Watch was the second choice.

The Derby lineup included two maidens—Patches (0 for 8) and Bersagliere (0 for 3)—and one horse who was making his first start of the year, Sterling. Cleopatra, the best three-year-old filly of 1920, also was in the starting cast.

Beginning with the 1920 renewal, weights for the Derby have remained the same for each subsequent running—126 for colts and geldings, 121 for fillies. Had Paul Jones come along a year earlier for the 1919 Derby, he would have carried 119 pounds, the impost for geldings before the 1920 change.

The value of the Derby was increased in 1920 to make it a $30,000-added event, richest in the race's first forty-six runnings. For winning this one race, Paul Jones took home $30,375, almost equaling the amount of money that he would earn for all the other starts—sixty-four of them—in his career.

It was a big-money day all around, the 1920 Derby. By the time the last dollar was put through the pari-mutuel windows that day, the Downs had realized its first million-dollar afternoon. A total of $1,055,191 was bet on the seven races.

For the Derby, the fifth race, Garth gave Ted Rice, who rode Paul Jones, and Clarence Kummer, the jockey for Blazes, brief instructions. "Just get away from the barrier as

Ted Rice, the jockey on 1920 Kentucky Derby winner Paul Jones. (Photo courtesy Keeneland-Cook)

quickly as possible," he said, "and if you get in front, don't let the others catch you."

Paul Jones, ready for the race of his life, came out of the paddock with his head high, tugging at the bit. He broke from the number-two post position, Blazes from number fifteen.

The track was just right for Paul Jones, a son of Sea King. If John Paul Jones was the "Father of the American Navy," then Paul Jones was right at home on the Derby's wet racetrack, which was listed as slow.

As the field was sent on its way, Parr nervously fingered his binoculars. "Paul has started," he muttered to a member of his party.

Paul Jones went to the front at once, just as many suspected he would in his expected role as a rabbit for Blazes. But rather than set the race up for a stretch surge by Blazes, Paul Jones stayed in front. Upset made a strong run at Paul Jones in the final quarter of a mile. Near the sixteenth pole, the shout rang out from some in the crowd that Upset was going to win. But Parr was confidently clamoring for his horse. "He'll do it! He'll do it!" he cried out. "He'll do it! He'll do it!

"He's done it!"

Paul Jones had hung on by a head or a neck or half a length, depending on which account you believe.

On Watch, ahead of only one opponent at the start call in the seventeen-horse cavalry charge, rallied to finish third. Overcoming interference in his come-from-behind surge, On Watch appeared to be a serious threat rounding the final turn. "On Watch wins!" shouted one veteran horseman. The game colt moved up to third at the stretch call, just a neck off the lead, but couldn't sustain his charge and ended up four lengths behind Upset at the wire.

Cleopatra, the filly, finished far back in fifteenth.

Oftentimes after a horse makes up ground in the home-stretch as Upset did, his supporters will argue that he would have won had the race been a little longer. But Rice didn't agree with the notion that Paul Jones would have been overtaken. "He did not win by a big margin," said the jockey, "but he was not all in by any means, and if we had had any further to go he would have been found fighting it out in front just the same, in my opinion."

Rice said Paul Jones had his running shoes on for the Derby. "It was just a case of let him run, once he got to the front, and, believe me, he wanted to run fast every inch of the way. I kept a snug hold on him while he was setting the early pace so that he would have some speed left for the stretch drive, and when I dropped him down making the turn for home he drew away from his field with ease. I took no chances with him and shook him up a bit after passing the eighth pole, and he responded just like I figured he would."

Paul Jones traveled the first quarter in :23$\frac{4}{5}$, followed by the next three quarters in successively slower times—:24$\frac{2}{5}$, :26$\frac{3}{5}$, and :27$\frac{1}{5}$. In the last quarter, he came home in :27, giving him a final time of 2:09. Only two Derbies since then have been run in slower time—2:10$\frac{2}{5}$ in 1928 and 2:10$\frac{4}{5}$ in 1929.

Immediately after his gelding won the Derby, Parr had difficulty reaching the winner's circle. "Lemme out! Lemme out!" he yelled, shoving his way through the crowd. "You people make room."

"Sit down, you boob!" screamed an angry spectator, unwilling to relinquish his spot on the rail between the clubhouse and judges' stand. "You can't tramp all over me! Losing your head because you've got a two-dollar ticket on the winner. Git away from this fence. This is my place."

"Lemme out, I tell you," insisted Parr. "I'm the owner of the horse that won the Derby." With that, he was given a hand and boosted over the fence.

Parr talked of the excitement of winning the Derby. "I'll never forget the thrill as my colors came down in front," he said. "I guess Paul Jones is a better horse than we thought. Anyway, Billy Garth deserves all credit.

"It is a grand and glorious feeling to be able to say that your horse won the Kentucky Derby, the most famous race in America, and I am certainly enjoying the feeling right now. I always had a lot of confidence in Paul Jones, and the way that he trained for the race made me real sweet on his chances to win the big stake. Naturally, I thought that Blazes, my other horse, was the best, but in my mind there was not a whole lot of difference between them. When I saw Paul Jones go to the front right at the outset, I knew that it was going to be a tough job to catch him—and so it proved. Blazes did not run a bad race, and I was highly pleased with his showing, especially since his stablemate won the Derby."

Parr had wagered on both Blazes and Paul Jones in Derby future-book betting. During the early spring of 1920, he bet on Paul Jones at odds of 100-1. Furthermore, the mere appearance of Blazes in the Derby meant $4,000 extra to Parr. It seems that the previous fall, a Kentucky turfman whose name wasn't revealed bet Parr that the colt would not make it to the post in the Derby. The Kentuckian put up $4,000 to Parr's $500.

Parr might have made a big score in Derby future-book betting, but he was one of the relatively few to hit the jackpot in this form of wagering. The Derby result enabled many bookmakers to breathe a sigh of relief. *The Louisville Times* noted:

> Paul Jones' victory saved the makers of future books thousands. Many of the local layers were calling for life preservers Friday night. They were whining and crying they were "dutched" on the Whitney horses and the Loft pair.

Parr parted with some of his money immediately after the Derby. Showing his appreciation, he gave Rice, the winning jockey, a gift of $5,000. Rice, in turn, split the $5,000 with

Kummer, who rode stablemate Blazes. Earlier in the day, Parr had told Rice and Kummer that he would reward the winner with $5,000. The two jockeys agreed to split such a prize down the middle in the event one of them triumphed.

The $5,000 was quite a fee. Indeed, it was reported that the $5,000 represented the largest sum ever given a jockey for riding a winner in Kentucky.

By winning a Kentucky Derby nowadays, a horse increases in value by millions of dollars, but not so with Paul Jones. As a gelding, he was worth only what he could pick up on the racetrack, and, once retired, his earning potential was over. In the wake of his Derby victory, a story noted, "It is the intention of Captain Parr and Mr. Cosden to eventually make a jumper out of Paul Jones, as both men are very fond of this branch of racing."

If the Paul Jones people couldn't look forward to cashing in on his future in retirement, at least one member of the stable—trainer Garth—was able to count on the benefits of breeding free of charge to the Derby winner's sire, Sea King. The day after the Derby, Garth received a telegram from Thomas Fortune Ryan, the owner of Sea King and master of Oak Ridge Farm in Virginia. Ryan, fully appreciating the training job done with Paul Jones, told Garth in the wire: "Congratulations. More will think as you and I do about Sea King. Kindly accept service of Sea King for the mares you and Lewis sent to Oak Ridge as complimentary." Eight mares owned by Garth and his son, Lewis, had been sent to Oak Ridge earlier that spring to be bred to Sea King.

Back home in Baltimore, Paul Jones' Derby victory was front-page news in *The Baltimore Sun.* "The name of Paul Jones has taken its rightful place among those of Aristides, Regret and Sir Barton, to live in that eternal abode of turf fame provided for victors of America's supreme classic," declared *The Sun.* "The forty-sixth Derby will be remembered as one of the greatest in [the] history of the sport."

Paul Jones and Blazes were shipped from Kentucky the day after the Derby, both bound for Pimlico. It was reported in Louisville that they were being pointed for the Preakness. But only Blazes started in the Pimlico race. C. Edward Sparrow wrote in *The Sun*:

> Baltimoreans can not pay homage to Paul Jones in the Preakness. The winner of the Kentucky Derby is not eligible. He is a gelding and a year or so ago the Maryland Jockey Club ruled out such horses in the big classic.

Of Garth, Sparrow wrote, "Billy is one of the most popular trainers on the turf and his ambition of winning the Derby finally has been realized."

Rice, the jockey for Paul Jones, was warmly cheered when he raced in Baltimore the Monday after the Derby. Sparrow wrote:

> No jockey ever received a greater homage than Rice at Old Hilltop. Super was his first mount, and as soon as he poked his head on the track the clubhouse fans began to applaud. The handclapping was taken up by the spectators in the grandstand, by those on the lawn, and later by the bleacherites. The applause continued until Rice had turned with the procession and was on his way to the six-furlong barrier. The fans wanted to show Rice their appreciation of his splendid ride on Paul Jones for a Baltimore turfman.

Incidentally, Rice rode Super to a 1½-length victory over Scurry, who represented the same Whitney stable that owned Derby runner-up Upset.

Paul Jones returned to the races a month after the Derby and won the 1¼-mile Suburban Handicap. Carrying 106 pounds and Andy Schuttinger, Paul Jones opened up a long lead and held on under punishment to edge Boniface by a head or half-length. Rice, who had earned acclaim for his Derby ride on Paul Jones, was aboard Exterminator in this race. With top weight of 123 pounds, Exterminator came in third, six lengths behind Boniface. The winning time in muddy going was 2:09⅗, all of 9⅗ seconds off the track record.

Reporting on the Suburban, *The New York Times* observed, "Captain Ral Parr's sturdy gelding, Paul Jones, proved to a storm-swept crowd of 10,000 at Belmont Park this his victory in the Kentucky Derby was by no means a fluke, and that he is entitled to rank high among the horses of his age." The race was run in "a sea of mud," the paper noted. "It was a track made to order for Paul Jones. . . . He just frolicked in the going as if to prove to the onlookers that the mud running trait which was so strongly a characteristic of his sire had been transmitted to him."

Following his Suburban victory, Paul Jones was sent back to Kentucky to run in the Latonia Derby, a race in which he was to carry high weight of 131 pounds. He reached Kentucky four days before the race. "He stood the long journey in fine style and was little the worse for it when unloaded," reported one newspaper.

But things didn't go well for Paul Jones this time in Kentucky. He suffered an injury training for the Latonia Derby. It was reported that he either "struck a stone or split a hoof in some manner." Paul Jones "was limping when he pulled up after his workout, but this is common with him, and Garth thought little of the matter until he got back to the stable and gave him a careful looking over," a dispatch to *The Courier-Journal* noted. "When he discovered the bruise he pulled off the shoe and put the horse's foot in a bucket of ice to take out the inflammation."

Commenting on the Latonia Derby, Walter H. Pearce of *The Louisville Times* wrote:

> In the Kentucky Derby, Upset was catching Paul Jones with every jump and it must be admitted that the Parr representative is pounds the best over a muddy course. These two colts [*sic*] seem much the best on

> past races, but there is a chance for Peace Pennant to cause an upset, as his last race was a sparkling performance and, if duplicated, would bring him close to the finishing line in front. Paul Jones is almost certain to be scratched.

If Pearce was wrong about Paul Jones' manhood, he was right about his starting status for the Latonia Derby. The gelding was scratched. On the morning of the Latonia Derby, *The Courier-Journal* reported:

> Trainer William Garth will ship Paul Jones back East Sunday if he can get an express and the gelding will be thrown out of training for the time being. He will be turned over to Dr. McCully, one of the best known veterinarians in the United States, upon his arrival in New York. This morning Garth put a bar plate on the Kentucky Derby winner's left front foot which is ailing him and he jogged a short distance without showing any visible signs of lameness. A short while later, however, he began to limp, and it was with difficulty that he was cooled out.

It wasn't until late in the summer that Paul Jones resumed racing. At Havre de Grace, he finished fourth and last in the Potomac Handicap, a 1¹⁄₁₆-mile race won in track-record time by Man o' War. Favored at fifteen cents on a dollar, Man o' War carried 138 pounds and finished 18½ lengths ahead of Paul Jones, who had 114 up.

Paul Jones lost four more races in Maryland before winning a 1¼-mile allowance at Laurel Park. His time of 2:07²⁄₅ on a racing strip listed as "good" was 5²⁄₅ seconds off the track record. Paul Jones, the favorite over four older opponents, captured this race by rushing to the front under Kummer's handling and staying there the entire way for a 1¼-length triumph.

The Paul Jones camp then bunched three races in just over a week's time for the gelding's final 1920 appearances. The three races were not for the fainthearted. They totaled five miles in length. Paul Jones finished fourth in the 1¼-mile Pimlico Autumn Handicap on November 4, fourth in the 1½-mile Bowie Handicap (run at Pimlico) on November 8, and third in the 2¼-mile Pimlico Cup Handicap on November 12. On Watch set a track record in winning the Pimlico Autumn Handicap, as did Exterminator in the Pimlico Cup Handicap. In the middle race, the Bowie Handicap, Paul Jones rallied from last place, moved up to second at the stretch call, but tired at the end.

Paul Jones raced a dozen times as a four-year-old, seven in the state of New York and five in Maryland. He came home a winner only once—the Susquehanna Handicap at Havre de Grace. Bidding for a repeat victory in the Suburban Handicap, Paul Jones failed miserably. He came in dead last. He didn't distinguish himself in the Brooklyn Handicap either, running tenth, or the Manhattan Handicap, a fifth-place finish.

After being away from action for more than thirteen months, Paul Jones finally embarked on his five-year-old campaign on October 7, 1922. His stable made up for lost time in a hurry. In a three-week period, he started six times. That's right, *six* times, an average of two races a week. He was fifth October 7, second October 10, first October 17, last October 21, third October 26, and next-to-last October 28. His triumph on October 17, in a mile allowance, ended the longest losing streak of his career—eleven races.

Paul Jones was kept busy the next month, too, starting seven times, the first four at Pimlico, the next three at Bowie. He was third in the Stafford Handicap on November 1 and fifth five days later in the Forest Park Handicap. The very next day, on November 7, after hardly enough time to catch his breath, Paul Jones started again. He rallied to finish fourth at 24-1 odds in the 1½-mile Bowie Handicap (run at Pimlico).

On November 11, he ran second in the 2¼-mile Pimlico Cup Handicap. Carrying 99 pounds, he finished a length and a half back of Captain Alcock and some thirty lengths in front of Exterminator, highweighted at 126 pounds.

Paul Jones then received a breather. He didn't race the next eight days (some breather). He won in that next start, a 1 1/16-mile allowance, beating the odds-on Prudery by a length. Five days later, Paul Jones was fifth in the Prince George Handicap, and then on November 30 he dragged himself home tenth in the Thanksgiving Day Handicap. Blazes came in far back himself on Thanksgiving Day, finishing twelfth, nine lengths behind Paul Jones.

In less than eight weeks during the fall of 1922, Paul Jones' people had managed to crowd together thirteen races totaling almost 15 3/16 miles in distance for this five-year-old gelding. It makes you wonder if they couldn't have found time to have him pull a milk wagon around Baltimore during his days off from the races.

Paul Jones launched his six-year-old season in the spring of 1923 with a victory in a mile-and-seventy-yard allowance. Five days later, he finished second to Exterminator in the Philadelphia Handicap and the next week ran third in the Old Dominion Handicap. After those first three races of 1923 at Havre de Grace, Paul Jones made his next start at Pimlico and ran second as the odds-on favorite in the Stafford Handicap.

Taken to the Big Apple, Paul Jones lost five straight races, four at Belmont Park and one at Aqueduct, although he finished in the money in four of those starts.

From New York, Paul Jones then raced in Chicago for the first time. He failed in his two initial races at Hawthorne, running his losing streak to ten races.

Paul Jones returned to the winner's circle for the last time in his long career on July 13, 1923. It was Friday the thirteenth, but the day was anything but unlucky for Paul Jones. Ridden by Eddie Ambrose and carrying a feathery 106 pounds, he won the Illinois Athletic Club Purse, an allowance race at Hawthorne. Paul Jones, who earned $900, won the mile event in 1:38⅖ on a fast racing strip, just two-fifths of a second off the track record. *Daily Racing Form*'s chart erroneously listed his breeder as J. C. Milam.

Milam owned Exterminator early in his career, and, as things turned out, four days after Paul Jones' final victory, the six-year-old gelding ran in a mile race called the Exterminator Purse. He ran even faster this time than he had in his previous start, but it wasn't fast enough to win. Rallying from last place in a field of seven, Paul Jones appeared to some observers to have triumphed, but it was ruled that Actuary had edged him. Actuary, a three-year-old colt, was timed in 1:37⅕, clipping four-fifths of a second off the Hawthorne track record.

Paul Jones finished his career by racing twice at Saratoga. He ran fifth in both races, which were won by My Play, the full brother of Man o' War. For his final start, which came in the Uncas Handicap, Paul Jones "had no mishaps," according to the footnotes in *Daily Racing Form*'s chart.

Paul Jones had no mishaps in that race, but the same couldn't be said a month and a half later for his Kentucky Derby jockey, Ted Rice. On October 6, 1923, Rice was killed in a spill at Jamaica. His mount, McKee, bolted and crashed through the inside rail. "His skull was fractured and he was cut about the face and never regained consciousness," reported *The New York Times*.

The paper went into detail in describing the accident:

> Without warning and for no cause that was discovered after the accident, McKee swerved sharply and bolted squarely into the rail. The heavy rail was broken about in the middle and Rice was catapulted from the saddle, his head striking the jagged end of the split rail. Both horse and rider crashed into the starter's stand at that point and demolished it.
>
> Rice lay where he fell, his head resting in the draining ditch inside the rail. The splinters of the rail had crushed through the skull and penetrated the brain.

McKee got to his feet, clear of the prostrate jockey,
before any one could reach them. His off foreleg was
broken and nearly torn off and he was later destroyed.

Rice's mother witnessed the tragedy. She fainted and,
with difficulty, was finally revived. Among the thirty-two-year-
old jockey's other survivors was a baby who had been born
just two weeks earlier.

Parr, whose silks Paul Jones carried in the Derby, died
October 10, 1939, at the age of sixty-two. Horses had been
in his blood throughout his life. As *The Maryland Horse* magazine put it in his obituary, he was a born horseman who
"early took up riding and driving, beginning with a goat,
going through successive stages to donkeys, ponies, and
show horses, finally achieving the crowning experience of
his career, by breeding and owning one of the crack two-
year-olds of this season, Victory Morn."

Parr was a major engaged in the Army Remount Service
during World War I. A patron of the arts and music, he was
one of the founders of the old Baltimore Horse Show
Association.

According to *The Maryland Horse*, "he not only exhibited
and rode his mounts in the ring, but was an exceptionally
good four-in-hand whip, his teams being always faultlessly
turned out; he also hunted with the Elkridge and Green
Spring Valley Hounds."

As a director of the Maryland Jockey Club, Parr took an
active hand in urging improvements that upgraded Pimlico
and established it as one of the most up-to-date tracks in
America. He also was a highly respected official with the
Maryland Horse Breeders' Association.

Parr started only two horses—Paul Jones and Blazes—in
the Derby, but the Baltimore man had five representatives
in his hometown's classic, the Preakness. Those five were
the Governor (who finished fourth in 1914), the entry of
Nebraska and the Belgian II (seventh and thirteenth,
respectively, in 1917), Blazes (sixth, 1920), and Hypocrite
(eighth, 1938).

Paul Jones, who completed his career with fourteen victories, twelve seconds, and thirteen thirds in his sixty-five starts, spent about the last half of his life in the care of another owner, Mrs. John Porter Jones. Mrs. Jones, popularly known as "Miss Berta," was a daughter of Billy Garth, the trainer of Paul Jones. Her husband, well known as "Doc" Jones, was a physician who turned to training horses.

Paul Jones "went lame and had to be nerved," Mrs. Howard Y. Haffner, the daughter of the Joneses, once recalled. "They were going to destroy him or something." However, rather than have Paul Jones put down, Mrs. Jones asked for the horse, who was turned over to her.

"My father schooled him and rode him in pink-coat races [informal steeplechase races], gentleman races, and hunt races around," Mrs. Haffner said many years later. "And then mother hunted him sidesaddle. She rode sidesaddle always. He was a family horse, really."

Mrs. Haffner used to ride Paul Jones herself. "I was young, but I rode him. He was quiet, a very smart, sensible horse. He was a brown horse with a white face and four white feet."

Paul Jones was destroyed at the age of thirteen due to physical infirmities. He was buried at the Inglecress Farm, Charlottesville, Virginia. No monument was placed over his grave, but a fitting epitaph would have been: *Paul Jones (1917-30) . . . He raced long, hard, and often . . . and always gave his best.*

Whiskey. (Photo courtesy Keeneland-Cook)

14

Whiskery—an Old Soldier

WHISKERY, THE 1927 Kentucky Derby winner, was like an old soldier. He didn't die. He just faded away.

As can best be determined, no lasting record of this famous racehorse's death was made. Fifty years after Whiskery's Derby victory, I started checking around in an attempt to find out when the old horse died. His death was never reported to The Jockey Club . . . the Keeneland Library was unable to uncover the year of his demise . . . *The Blood-Horse* and *The Thoroughbred Record* magazines had no information pertaining to his death. Neither did *Daily Racing Form*. Whiskery won the Derby for Harry Payne Whitney, and the Lexington farm of his son, C. V., similarly has no record of the horse's death. Ceaseless research by the Keeneland Library turned up a book that referred to Whiskery's demise, and a telephone call to Morven Stud in Virginia produced another source. Still, neither source was specific about the year that Whiskery passed away.

Whiskery was sold in 1928 by Whitney to the three-man partnership of Charlie Stone, A. B. Hancock, and William Woodward, Sr. Stone had a half-interest in the horse, Woodward and Hancock each a quarter. In *From Here to the Bugle,* a book about the Hancock family, Frank Jennings wrote that Whiskery sold for $60,000 "and by the time the insurance and other incidentals were paid the total expense was considerably above that."

Big things were expected of Whiskery in the stud, but unfortunately he turned out to be sterile. Seeking to recoup at least part of their investment, his owners put him back in training.

"He was sulky and so they gelded him, hoping to cure this bothersome habit, but it did little good," Jennings wrote.

Whiskery likewise turned out to be a failure as a runner for his new owners, and Woodward and Hancock decided to give their shares in the horse to Stone. Retired from racing with fourteen victories in seventy career starts, Whiskery was shipped to Stone's Morven Stud in Charlottesville, Virginia, during the summer of 1931. The idea was to use him as a saddle horse. "This didn't work out so well, either," Jennings wrote. "He was injured while running in his pasture one day and had to be destroyed."

Providing more details about Whiskery's days at Morven Stud was the other source—Charlie Stone's son, Whitney Stone, who remembered the horse. He should have. He used to ride him around the farm.

"We brought him up here, and we didn't know what the hell to do with him," Stone, owner of Morven Stud, said in a 1977 interview. "So I rode him around the place. I used to have a nice time just riding him around. He was a perfectly good old horse to ride."

But Stone noted that Whiskery had a bad leg that was getting a little worse. "So I didn't ride him much more. We turned him into a night-watchman's horse. But the horse kept running into things, like bushes and trees and stuff . . . and he poked his eye out and he then hit a tree with one leg and we finally put him down.

"I can't tell you what date it was," Stone added. "I haven't any foggy notion. I was a kid." Apparently, though, it was around 1936 because Stone did note that Whiskery was at Morven Stud about five years before he was put down.

Whiskery wasn't buried, Stone said. "There's nothing to identify where he is or what happened or anything."

If the horse had been buried, Stone himself said something in the interview that would have been a fitting epitaph
on a tombstone. "He was a great old horse." It would be better to remember Whiskery that way than to think of this
Kentucky Derby winner who was ridden to his famous victory by Linus ("Pony") McAtee winding up as nothing more
than a saddle horse, one who was relegated to be ridden at
the end by a night watchman.

It was a sad windup to his life, but at least Whiskery did
accomplish something during his racing days that stamped
him indelibly in the sport's history. He won the Kentucky
Derby. Let's flip back the pages of history to 1927, splicing
in some interviews with old-timers, and take a look at that
Derby.

In 1927, the racing calendar was somewhat different than
today. The Preakness back then, for example, was run on
Monday, May 9, five days before the Kentucky Derby. The
Pimlico classic was won by Bostonian, also owned by Harry
Payne Whitney, with Whiskery finishing third.

The Derby Trial, which was run on May 7, was won by
Rolled Stocking, who scored by six lengths over the favored
Osmand, ridden by Earl Sande. Willie Pool, who rode
Rolled Stocking, had a vivid recollection of that race. "I was
just sitting there choking my horse," he said in a 1975 interview. "Old man Van [trainer Charlie Van Meter] said, 'I
don't want you to go to the front on this horse till you hit
the head of the stretch.' And I was scared I was gonna
choke him 'cause he was a high-headed horse and he'd run
with his head real high. And those kind of horses are easy
to choke.

"And so I come to the head of the stretch, and I was sure
glad to see that quarter pole 'cause I'm pullin' him out in
the middle of the racetrack. Man, he just flew. Well, Sande
come out after me. He come out after me and he *had* me.
He just wrapped that leg around me about the eighth pole.
He was the best leg-lockin' rider ever lived. And, of course, I

got out of it. I got unhooked. I was on so much the best horse.

"I went back to the jocks' room, and they had to grab me. I had grabbed a bootjack, and I went after him [Sande]. And I don't know what I'da did if he happen to beat me. But they grabbed me and they stopped it all."

Osmand, a big gelding who ruled as the Derby's future-book favorite, had sustained a punctured foot by picking up a rusty nail some two weeks before the classic, and at first it was feared the injury might prove to be serious. Though he made a rapid recovery, some observers later chose to use the injury as an excuse for his Derby loss, citing the time that he had missed from training. Others, however, contended that Osmand had recuperated quickly enough and that it wasn't the nail—but rather his lack of stamina—that cost him the Derby.

Veterinarian Henry Harthill of Louisville treated Osmand for that injury, the second straight year that he had put his hands on a horse that was heavily bet in the future books. In 1926, Harthill had doctored the heralded Carlaris, who was suffering with a hock injury. To the disappointment of those who made future-book bets on him, Carlaris didn't start in the Derby. But Osmand did.

Horses were tougher in those days, and Osmand, following his loss in the Derby Trial, came back just three days before the big race to win the 1¹⁄₁₆-mile Watterson Hotel Purse by a nose under a masterful ride by Sande. Jock finished second.

Whiskery was ridden in the Preakness by Clarence Kummer, but he was set down by the Pimlico stewards for roughriding on the next day's card, the suspension costing him a chance to ride the Whitney colt in the Derby. It initially was reported that Mark Fator would replace Kummer as Whiskery's rider in the Derby, but McAtee ended up with the mount.

A crowd, overestimated at more than seventy-five thousand, turned out for the Derby and sent the entry of

Whiskery and Bostonian off as the favorite. Included in the throng was a Louisville railroad man named J. B. Hitt. Hitt saw more than seventy Derbies in his lifetime, and the 1927 renewal was unique to him in one respect. He bet on every horse in the race, the only time he ever did that.

Hitt was hoping mainly that Whiskery or Bostonian would win the Derby, but he wagered on the rest of the starters as insurance. "I bet enough on Whiskery that I quit about a $150 winner on the race," he recalled. "I had at least $2 on every horse."

Hitt somehow obtained a press pass for that Derby and watched the race from atop the roof. "The newsreel reporters were located there, taking the pictures of the race," he said.

There was somebody else on the roof that afternoon. Would you believe, a person actually booking bets? "There was a man up there with a roll of money that would choke a horse, taking any and all bets that you might want to make on the races—not only for the Derby but for all the rest of the races," Hitt said. "And the reason for that in my opinion was that everybody was busy and didn't have a chance to go down to make their bets or didn't go down to make them and this man was just booking the bets on the roof."

Imagine that! Illegal bookmaking was taking place on the hallowed grounds of Churchill Downs. And if you let your imagination absolutely run wild, you might even conjure up thoughts of a person slipping past the Churchill Downs security force that day with a flask in his pocket, completely disregarding the Eighteenth Amendment.

As far as some people were concerned, Churchill Downs was brimming with sin. "'A riot of gambling' is characterization of the Kentucky Derby, by the Seventy-second Southern Baptist Convention, which could be upheld, no doubt, by an investigator looking for sinfulness at Churchill Downs," *The Louisville Times* stated in a Derby Week editorial. "But the proportion of sinners at the Derby is not as large as some persons might suppose, unless one holds the extreme view that laying $5 on a horse race once a year for mere amusement is sinful."

Veteran Louisville newspaperman Mike Barry saw sixty-six Derbies over the years, and the most vivid memory he had of the 1927 renewal is the long lead that Jock had. It was the longest lead that he had ever seen a horse take in all his years of watching the classic. "The chart doesn't show him that far in front, but Jock had to be ten lengths in front around the half-mile pole," Barry said. "It might have been the longest lead *ever* in the Derby."

Jock, who was destined to finish third under jockey Chick Lang's handling, began to lose that lengthy lead, and, when he did, Sande was ready to overtake him with Osmand. That wasn't all Sande was ready to do.

In Sande's opinion, the finest ride he ever gave a horse came in the 1927 Derby with Osmand, who actually didn't have the ability to win at a mile and a quarter against top competition. Yet thanks to Sande's skills, the Joseph E. Widener color-bearer almost won the Derby. He lost by just a head to Whiskery.

Sande, a gifted roughrider, was at his best in this race. And when he got close enough to Jock with Osmand, he went to work. Frank Coltiletti, who rode Scapa Flow to a ninth-place finish in the '27 Derby, remembered well the shenanigans pulled off by Sande. "Sande was givin' that poor Chick Lang an awful going-over," Coltiletti recalled. "He was grabbin' him and messin' around with him and doin' everything to him, and the first thing you know, McAtee run by him with Whiskery."

The way jockey Willie Garner recalled the race, McAtee had considerable difficulty before he could get past Sande in the homestretch. "I was right behind him, and he done everything in the world to McAtee," said Garner, who finished fourth aboard Hydromel. "He grabbed him, he leg locked him, and everything else in the stretch. And he grabbed McAtee's stirrup about seventy yards from the finish, and I thought McAtee was gonna fall off. McAtee come back to the jocks' room, and he told Sande, 'It's a good thing I win it or I'da killed you sure as hell.'"

Peter Burnaugh of the *New York Sun* heaped praise on McAtee for his ride. "McAtee, riding his first race on a Whitney horse since he left the employ of the stable last year, showed what a good jockey Trainer [James] Rowe lost when he let the boy go," Burnaugh wrote after the Derby. "If a slightly less cool or less skilled rider than McAtee had been on Whiskery, Osmand and Earl Sande would have given Mr. Widener his first Kentucky Derby."

Whiskery, a lithe, long-necked brown colt, covered the Derby's mile and a quarter in 2:06 on a track rated as slow. His time for the final quarter of a mile was an unimpressive 27 seconds, but it was still good enough to get him past the faltering Jock near midstretch and the tired Osmand at the wire.

In winning, Whiskery ended a Derby drought for his owner. Since his Regret triumphed in 1915, Whitney had run sixteen losers in the Derby from 1916 to 1926. One of those losers was Whiskery's dam, Prudery, who finished third in 1921 behind Behave Yourself and Black Servant, both owned by Col. E. R. Bradley.

In the paddock before the 1927 Derby, Colonel Bradley made it clear how he thought the race would go when he was asked by Van Meter, the trainer of Rolled Stocking, which horse he thought would win. "Max Hirsch will win with Rip Rap," Bradley declared.

"Who's gonna come in second?" Van Meter asked.

"I'll be second with Bewithus," Bradley replied.

"Well, Colonel," Van Meter said, "you don't give my horse much chance."

"No, Charlie, I don't give your horse much chance," Bradley said straightforwardly.

Bradley was right about Rolled Stocking. The best he could do was twelfth. Bradley likewise was right about Bewithus finishing directly behind Rip Rap: it was Rip Rap thirteenth, Bewithus fourteenth.

Rolled Stocking, second choice in the betting, actually had an excuse for his poor showing. "When the gate went up, I broke *real* good and I was to lay fourth till the half-a-mile pole," said Pool, his rider. "And when we got to the half-mile pole, I didn't know it, but this horse had turned his shoe. A horse had stepped on him leavin' the gate, clipped his hoof and grabbed that shoe, and caused it to turn to sit sideways.

"And I'm layin' fourth, and at the half-mile pole, I went to move on him. That shoe was hittin' the inside leg and he couldn't stand the pain any longer and he just sorts bolted with me. Bolted at the half-mile pole and I thought I was gonna go through that kitchen there at the half-mile pole.

"And they had a water wagon sittin' there at the head of the stretch on the outside, and I didn't miss that water wagon two foot. I never will forget that. I knew there was something wrong with him. Of course, he wasn't lame or nothin', but I knew there was something wrong with him, and I just pulled him up. And when we came back, why, old man Van Meter, man, he was hot. He was a hard man to ride for anyway. And I told him, 'I don't know what happened, Mr. Van.'

"So before I could get out of that jocks' room, he'd come and met me at the jocks' room. He said, 'It wasn't your fault. That horse twisted a shoe. And that's what caused it.'

"So there's a case where if he'da lost his shoe, I think I'da win it."

The Thoroughbred Record reported on the presentation ceremony in this fashion:

> The usual ceremony of decorating the winner with flowers accompanied by the clicking of cameras and turning the cranks of the movie machies having gotten over, William Hale Thompson, Mayor of Chicago, presented the golden trophy to the proud and happy Freddy Hopkins, trainer of Whiskery. Mr. H.P. Whitney, who came from New York to attend the Derby, was deprived of the thrill of seeing his colors

carried to victory in the race. Mr. Whitney made the trip suffering with a severe cold and when the early shower of the afternoon developed he left the course and returned to his private car, fearing to subject himself to the untoward weather conditions.

Whitney, in his absence from the Derby, deputized his son, C. V., known as "Sonny," to accept the trophy and make a speech on the presentation stand in the event that the stable won.

At the track that day, C. V. wound up at lunchtime in a crowded dining room, seated at a table with three strangers. One of them was none other than Ring Lardner, who had invited Whitney to have a seat at the table.

Whitney got around to telling Lardner that he was a newcomer to racing, that his father wanted him to say something if Whiskery or Bostonian won, and that he didn't know what to say.

Lardner knew what Whitney should say. Mindful of the mud on the track, Lardner wrote on Whitney's cuff: "He won because his mudder was a mudder."

Whitney didn't make that statement afterward, or any statement, for that matter. In the hectic postrace activity, Whitney failed to reach the presentation stand. He got caught in the moving mass of people departing from the scene, and, rather than fight them he joined them, and some twenty minutes later he ended up outside the track.

Later that evening at the farm, Whitney witnessed a celebration that would leave him with a lasting impression. "I saw a bonfire on top of one of the hills," he once recalled. "And there were at least a hundred blacks gathered around singing spirituals."

As he drew closer, he could see a horse standing silhouetted against the light of the bonfire, and the farm's black workers, gathered around the horse, were singing. The curious Whitney turned to the man who had guided him to the hill and asked about the horse. "Why, Mister Sonny," the old man said, "that's Regret."

He explained to Whitney that Regret had been taken out of her stall and the workers were singing to her as a way of expressing their joy over winning the Derby with a horse from the farm. Whitney walked closer to the circle to listen to the singing. "I just stood there and watched as the music of the old spirituals filled the night air, and Regret stood like a statue, as if aware of what was happening."

That's the way it was . . . Derby Day in 1927.

15

Horses Have
Their Own Personalities

HORSES, LIKE PEOPLE, HAVE PERSONALITIES. Some are malicious while others are playful. Some are outgoing, while others prefer to remain in the background. Some have Type A personalities, others Type B. Trainer John T. Ward, Jr., perhaps put it best in 1995 when he described his entry in the Kentucky Derby—Pyramid Peak and Jambalaya Jazz, two completely different types of horses. "If you walked in a bar, Jambalaya Jazz would be sitting over in a corner booth sipping whiskey and Pyramid Peak would be up at the bar drinking beers with the gang."

Richard Stone Reeves, the most famous equine artist in the world, has painted many great horses since the 1940s, and he knows all about their dispositions. He calls Shergar, the 1981 Epsom Derby and Irish Derby winner, and Buckpasser, the 1966 Horse of the Year in North America, the friendliest horses he's ever painted.

Indeed, Shergar's personality may have led to his undoing. In February 1983, he was kidnapped from the Aga Khan's Ballymany Stud in Ireland, and in 1992 it was claimed that he had been shot a few hours after his abduction. "I think he was so friendly that I'm sure anybody could approach him and take him off," Reeves said in a 1996 interview. "He probably would have been willing to go with anybody. He probably would have been easily led off and put in a van and taken away. A lot of horses wouldn't stand for that. They don't like strangers. He seemed to like everybody. He liked children, too."

If Shergar was docile enough when he was first kidnapped, he became unruly shortly afterward, according to the 1992 claim (which may not have been entirely accurate). A police informer said Shergar was shot because he went into a frenzy in the unfamiliar surroundings and couldn't be controlled.

Buckpasser was "just a lovely horse," Reeves said. "And so was The Minstrel [the 1977 Epsom Derby champion]. They were just normally friendly animals, and they would let you come in the stall with them and always come over to you and greet you and sort of nuzzle you and make friends. Buckpasser's sire, Tom Fool, was a very nice horse, too. He was a very manageable and polite horse."

If Shergar, Buckpasser, and The Minstrel were extremely friendly, Halo is anything but an angel. This stallion stands at Stone Farm, the Paris, Kentucky, Thoroughbred nursery owned by Arthur B. Hancock III, and once when he was brought out for a posing session for Reeves, not one but two grooms were with him. "Arthur said, 'If you don't mind, we'll send two grooms out because this horse is pretty hard to handle,'" Reeves recalled. "And he really was hard to handle. They had a muzzle over his mouth at all times so that he wouldn't bite." Each groom held Halo by a shank, one on his left side and the other on his right—all the better to keep matters under control. Halo was sired by Hail to Reason, whom Reeves also painted. Reeves refers to Halo as "a mean horse" and Hail to Reason as "very rough . . . obviously, Halo inherited some of that."

But of all the horses Reeves has painted, a champion Standardbred by the name of Nevele Pride ranks as the roughest he's ever been around. "He was even worse than Halo." Two grooms each had a pole "to keep him from savaging them, and they *knew* him," Reeves said. "They were obviously scared to death of him. He did savage people. He'd not only bite them, he'd kick them. He'd really go after you. He was almost like a crazy horse." Reeves painted

Nevele Pride twice—as a racehorse and later as a stallion. "He got much worse as a sire," Reeves said.

Halo's mood, too, became worse as a sire. Mack Miller, who trained the horse throughout his career, referred to him as "a common son of a buck." Miller added, "In training, he wasn't as common as he was after he went to stud. When he was in training as a three-year-old in Aiken [South Carolina], on one or two occasions he dumped the rider and ran across the dirt road to John Gaver's stable. John called me one morning and said, 'Mack, if you don't control that black SOB, I'm going to shoot him.'"

Miller laughed at the recollection. "I don't know why I never cut him," said Miller, adding that he's glad he didn't have Halo gelded because the horse turned out to be "a very fine sire." Halo has sired two Kentucky Derby winners—Sunny's Halo (1983) and Sunday Silence (1989).

When mention is made of Kentucky Derby winners, the first horse many people think about is Secretariat. Secretariat wasn't camera shy. "People ask me why Secretariat was so special," said Ron Turcotte, who rode the handsome colt to victory in the 1973 Triple Crown. "First of all, he was a ham. When he'd hear a camera click or a camera rolling, he'd just pull up and look at the photographer, or he'd try to show off. I'd just let him do his thing. He knew what was going on.

"Secretariat loved people. He was a kind horse and a gorgeous horse. And I guess, with the Watergate scandal, people were looking for a hero. Secretariat was their hero."

Holy Bull, the 1994 Horse of the Year, was another popular horse who would pose quicker than you could say Marilyn Monroe. This gray runner proved to be one of the most popular horses in many years. His name, his color, his natural ability—all of those things went together to make him a favorite with the fans. "He's the people's horse," his groom, Bob Coffey, said at Keeneland in the fall of 1994. "He's popular all over the country, no matter where you go. People come from all over the country just to watch him, to look at him. They call his name; they stand up and cheer for him. I've never seen anything like it. And he loves it. He loves to pose. When he hears a camera click, he'll stop and just stand there and pose."

If it would be possible to determine the friendliest horse ever to win the Derby, Unbridled certainly would rank among those at the head of the list. When the 1990 Derby winner was retired the following year, trainer Carl Nafzger said, "I'm gonna miss him a bunch. You don't have a good friend for a long time and then he goes home and you don't miss him. Unbridled is what you'd always want. You'd always want the perfect horse. He never did bite anybody, he never did kick anybody, he had a great attitude, he loved people, loved kids—and when you asked him to run, he ran. He'd always give us his race."

Nafzger will always remember Unbridled's personality. Unbridled "had just a great disposition," the veteran trainer recalled in a 1995 interview. "He thought kids were the greatest thing in the world. There were more kids on his back than there were jockeys. He loved it."

Nafzger, who has long considered himself "a horse psychiatrist," emphasizes the importance of the mental approach in his profession. He wrote in his book, *Traits of a Winner: The Formula for Developing Thoroughbred Racehorses:*

> A winning racehorse must be mentally tough. . . .
> Unfortunately, horses by their very nature are not
> "mentally tough" creatures. Their nature is to flee from
> stressful situations rather than stay around and deal
> with the circumstances. Mental toughness in horses is
> relative. To be successful, a racehorse must have more
> mental toughness than the average horse. But even the
> horse which has a higher level of mental toughness
> must have as much mental stress eliminated from its
> life as possible.

A horse's disposition can determine what kind of runner he or she turns out to be. Forty Niner, the champion two-year-old colt of 1987 and runner-up in the 1988 Derby, "had a wonderful disposition," said Claiborne Farm president

Seth Hancock, "and I think that's probably what made him get a mile and a quarter because he was an awful fast horse, and with him being by Mr. Prospector, I guess you would have wondered how far he might have wanted to go. But he relaxed so well—not only during his races but before the races. He never wasted an ounce of energy except when they opened those doors [at the starting gate]."

Certain horses carry themselves as if they know that they are special. Such was Majestic Prince, the 1969 Derby winner. "Majestic Prince was the best-named horse there ever was unless he would have been named Majestic King," veterinarian Gary Lavin said. "He'd stand at the front of that stall, and he stood with his head up kinda high and he had an air about him that he *knew* he was a good horse. And he had a royal demeanor about him. He wasn't any trouble to work around, but you had to let him know that you were there and that you meant business. He was a playful kind of colt."

Sir Barton, who came along fifty years earlier to win the 1919 Triple Crown, was anything but playful. This horse was an "irascible, exasperating creature" who at times was "downright evil," wrote J. K. M. Ross, son of Sir Barton's owner, in his book, *Boots and Saddles.* "Sir Barton took no personal interest whatsoever in his own kind, and he completely ignored and apparently despised all human beings—with the possible exception of his groom, a huge and very dark-skinned Negro by the name of 'Toots' Thompson. Toots worshipped his charge, and I don't think he would have changed jobs with anyone."

Omaha, the 1935 Triple Crown champion, spent the latter part of his life at the Nebraska farm of Grove Porter. His son, J. Morton Porter, once recalled that "Big Red," the nickname he applied to Omaha, was "a bit cranky in his last months, but he was really interesting, with a personality all his own. One below-zero morning he bit my upper arm through several layers of heavy clothing. It did not break the skin, but my arm was black and blue, indicating the tremendous strength in his jaws."

Aristides, the inaugural 1875 Kentucky Derby winner purchased as a stallion by J. Lucas Turner of Missouri, reportedly wasn't the type of horse a person would like to spend a lot of time with in his stall. "What was reported of Aristides after Turner bought him is suspected of being embellished, as interest in him grew years later because of the rising fame of the Derby," Edward L. Bowen once wrote in *The Blood-Horse* magazine. "It was claimed at one point that his drop in value from the $20,000 he was said to be worth at the conclusion of his racing was due to his evil disposition; one dead groom, and several maimings and cripplings were attributed to him, but that is the sort of story which can grow from a single nipped hand—or from nothing concrete at all."

Ribot was another one of those horses whose disposition changed when he went to stud. The English-bred runner, who gained recognition as the greatest Italian racehorse of all time, won all sixteen of his career starts (1954-56). "Throughout his racing career, Ribot was an intelligent, quiet, well-behaved horse," William G. Munn wrote in the March 1, 1991 issue of *Thoroughbred Times.* "During his stud career, however, he became difficult, and at times his behavior could only be described as bizarre."

Ribot, who started his stud career in Europe, came to Darby Dan Farm in June 1960 and spent the rest of his days at that Lexington, Kentucky, Thoroughbred establishment. "People used to suggest that we get a goat or somethin' and put it in Ribot's stall to keep him quiet," the late Darby Dan manager Olin Gentry once recalled. "My answer to that question was you'd have to order 'em by the carload. Ribot would have killed them. He never tried to hurt anybody but himself, but if you'd put a goat in there, god durn, he'd climb the wall and stand up on his hind legs to chew out the top of the damn rafters in the barn." As a stallion, Ribot clearly wasn't the kind of horse you'd take to preschool for a show-and-tell session.

16

The 1932 Derby:
The Year "Hoodoo King" Won

THE FIELD OF TWENTY HORSES paraded onto the track at Churchill Downs on May 7, 1932, the afternoon of the Kentucky Derby. The temperature reached a high of eighty-three, and the sky was partly cloudy. Hopes were high among owners, trainers, and jockeys alike. Little did some of those participants know that a dark cloud would hang over them or their horses after that race.

At least eight jockeys who rode in the race would die tragically and/or prematurely. Five horses would come out of the Derby with injuries. Only four of the starters would ever capture a stakes after 1932, and three horses would never even win a race after running for the roses. It was a depression year, and post-Derby developments were quite depressing, particularly for certain jockeys in the race.

Burgoo King, the 1932 Derby winner, was named in honor of James T. Looney, a Lexington man famous for preparing Kentucky burgoo for outdoor gatherings. History would tell us that this horse who wore Derby saddlecloth number thirteen should have been called Hoodoo King.

Consider: Of the four jockeys to ride Burgoo King during his career, at least two committed suicide—Laverne Fator and Gilbert Elston, both in 1936. His Derby jockey, Louisvillian Eugene James, reportedly drowned accidentally, although rumor had it that it might not have been accidental. And the gifted, but controversial, Don Meade had his career damaged by run-ins with racing authorities.

James' body was pulled from Lake Michigan on June 11, 1933. He was a mere nineteen. Certain stories stated that James died in the water of shock or a heart attack. "James was one of the finest jockeys in the country until ill health interrupted his career," reported one newspaper. "He had planned to get into condition to ride this fall, according to Louisville relatives." His death certificate stated that he died from "suffocation due to drowning" and that he "was in the lake swimming and evidently became exhausted and drowned."

Even though the certificate termed his death accidental, rumors persisted that perhaps it wasn't. One longtime racing man said he had heard that James killed himself. "He had a lot of talent, a lot of promise, and he committed suicide by drowning himself," the man said.

Some old-timers recalled that the underworld allegedly was responsible for James' death. Said one man: "There was a big hole in the back of his head. They never investigated it. At that time, them was the rough days." Said another: "The rumor was that the Mafia put him away. He was a helluva rider, just a young kid. God knows how good a rider he'da been."

Fator, whom certain old-timers considered the greatest jockey in the sport's history, plunged to his death from a window at Jamaica Hospital. He had been suffering from intermittent attacks of delirium, caused by the pain of septic appendicitis. In his delirious state of mind, he had reridden races hour after hour. Nurses were startled by his shrill cries: "Get 'em, Scapa! Get 'em, Scapa Flow! Pompey, c'mon, Pompey!" Fator later asked a nurse to bring him some medicine. Upon her return to the room, she found his bed empty. Fator was lying in a courtyard some thirty feet below. He died of a skull fracture.

Elston committed suicide in Louisville in 1936. Having earlier suffered several bad spills that short-circuited his promising career, he reportedly was despondent because of excessive weight, liquor, and bad checks.

Fator and Elston joined James among jockeys who had 1932 Derby mounts. There were at least five other ill-fated riders in that race.

• Mack Garner died in 1936 only hours after winning once in four rides at River Downs. His nephew, Willie Garner, a jockey himself in the old days, once recalled, "The undertaker told us there was a blood clot—could have happened a month before, could have happened ten years before, maybe from some fall he had or somethin'—and when that got to his heart, it just stopped his heart, this blood clot."

• George Woolf, "The Iceman," was killed as a result of a 1946 spill at Santa Anita Park.

• Pete Walls, who rode the favored Tick On in the '32 Derby, died of injuries suffered in a baseball game at Saratoga Springs, New York.

• Earl Sande, a three-time Derby winner, died in 1968 in oblivion in an Oregon nursing home. A pathetic figure, he was sick and broke at the end.

• And then there was another sad story, that of Lavelle ("Buddy") Ensor. He possessed so much riding skill that trainer Thomas Healey declared, "Ensor had no equal as a jockey." But following a brilliant start as a jockey, Ensor gambled away his money and turned into an alcoholic. After he was denied a license for a number of years, he returned to riding in 1932. In 1947, a person spotted a thin, little man lying dead in a cemetery, not far from the Jamaica track. Some time later in the Queens General Hospital morgue the body was identified as that of Ensor. Destitute, he died of lobar pneumonia. In the latter years of his life, he had been arrested on vagrancy and disorderly conduct charges in Queens.

Five of those 1932 Derby jockeys—Fator, Garner, Woolf, Sande, and Ensor—were enshrined in the Official National Thoroughbred Racing Hall of Fame in Saratoga Springs.

None of the horses who ran in the '32 Derby made it to the Hall of Fame, but Top Flight did. This fifty-eighth Derby would have been a much better race had it attracted Top Flight, as well as Burning Blaze, Faireno, Universe, and Gusto.

Top Flight, a champion filly at two and three, was unbeaten in seven juvenile starts and compiled earnings of $219,000, the top figure for any horse in 1931 and a record for a two-year-old. Her earnings, which broke a record set in 1893 by Domino, weren't exceeded by another two-year-old until Native Dancer came along in 1952 to pile up $230,495.

Burning Blaze was recognized as the top two-year-old colt of 1931 and was the leading earner among juvenile males, with $83,625.

Faireno, the 1932 Belmont winner, shared acclaim with Burgoo King as the best three-year-old males of that season.

Universe won the Wood Memorial, which had produced the Kentucky Derby winner the previous two seasons (Gallant Fox, 1930, and Twenty Grand, 1931).

Gusto, who wasn't nominated to the Derby, developed into the leading money winner of 1932.

With those five at their best, the '32 Derby could have been something special. As it was, it was more of a consolation race than a championship affair.

Top Flight had her backers for the Derby, but Col. E. R. Bradley wasn't one of them. The owner of Burgoo King and Brother Joe offered to bet $20,000 to $10,000 that Top Flight wouldn't be among the Derby's in-the-money finishers.

Bradley, who loved to bet, was looking for all kinds of wagers before the '32 Derby. He arranged a bet with Chicagoan Pat Nash, one of the owners of Burning Blaze. Bradley took Burgoo King and Nash had Burning Blaze in a bet based on which horse would finish ahead of the other in the Derby.

Bradley also was said to have wagered heavily on Brother Joe in the Derby's future book. Moreover, he was willing to bet $5,000 that Burgoo King would beat any other three-year-old the first time they met as sophomores. No takers were forthcoming.

Top Flight and Faireno ran themselves out of the Derby picture in the Wood Memorial.

Top Flight represented C. V. Whitney, who was bidding to become the second owner to win the Derby with a filly. His father, Harry Payne Whitney, was the first, triumphing with Regret in 1915. The elder Whitney bred Top Flight but didn't live to see her race.

The Derby's future-book favorite, Top Flight had defeated the boys in three races as a two-year-old—the Saratoga Special, the Futurity Stakes at Belmont Park, and the Pimlico Futurity. Among her victims in both futurities was none other than Burgoo King. But in her first start at three, a week before the Derby, she finished a tired fourth as the Wood's 1-2 favorite. Her stable immediately scratched Louisville from her schedule.

As for Faireno, the Belair Stud colt ran eighth in the Wood, his second dismal effort in as many starts that season. So much for his Derby plans, too.

Burning Blaze and Universe made it to Louisville, but not to the Derby. Both were sidelined with injuries.

Burning Blaze, a colt with plenty of ability, debuted at three in the Seelbach Hotel Purse at Churchill Downs a week before the Derby. He won by 2½ lengths as the odd-on favorite. But he was cut down in the race, suffering a partially severed tendon in his left hind leg. Back at his barn, his grief-stricken people were literally crying. Their colt, who certain knowledgeable observers thought would have won the Derby, didn't resume racing for 2½ years. Upon his return, he raced twice. He finished last both times.

Looking back on Burning Blaze's mishap, his jockey, Willie Garner, once was quoted as saying, "He came to Churchill Downs in great shape, and we thought we had the winner. The colt was cut down and his career about destroyed. It was an out-and-out case of roughriding."

Burning Blaze and Burgoo King had met twice in their careers, both times at Laurel in the fall of their two-year-old seasons. Burning Blaze finished ahead of the Bradley colt in each race. Burning Blaze won the six-furlong Richard Johnson Stakes, finishing some 3¼ lengths ahead of fifth-place Burgoo King. Three weeks later, the favored Burning Blaze ran third in the one-mile Spalding Lowe Jenkins Handicap, 7½ lengths in front of Burgoo King, the second choice who finished seventh.

Universe suffered a wrenched coffin joint and a cracked heel either during or after a workout three days before the Derby. He was second choice in the Derby's future book at the time.

Gusto, sired by American Flag, was the year's number-one money winner with a bankroll of $145,940. His triumphs included The Jockey Club Gold Cup, American Derby, and Arlington Classic.

Some of those who ran in the Derby weren't in sound condition. The status of Liberty Limited was uncertain. He had been suffering from infected heels, but veterinarian Henry Harthill said early in Derby Week that the colt would start. He did, but he would have been better off staying in the barn.

Brother Joe was another who wasn't sound.

The Bradley stable, which was trying to run one-two in the Derby as it had done in 1921 (Behave Yourself and Black Servant) and 1926 (Bubbling Over and Bagenbaggage), gave its twosome of Burgoo King and Brother Joe plenty of work in the week leading up to the big race.

A week before the race, they trained a mile and a quarter. Leonard Hale rode Brother Joe, and Fator was up on Burgoo King. One worked in 2:11, the other in 2:11⅗, but stories weren't consistent as to which colt was faster. Both colts seemed to have something left on the muddy track.

On Tuesday, Burgoo King, piloted by Fator, and Brother Joe, with Hale up, breezed four furlongs in 48⅗ seconds as a team.

On Wednesday, the Bradley pair again worked the Derby distance. Burgoo King, ridden by Hale, covered the mile and one-quarter in 2:07⅗ or 2:08 handily. Brother Joe, with Fator aboard, went in 2:09 driving. The latter was sore in both forelegs coming off the track but walked out of it while cooling out.

On Derby Eve, Burgoo King and Brother Joe went five furlongs together in 1:01⅖. That same morning Tick On blew out three furlongs in a time that ranged from 33⅗ to 35 seconds on various watches. "I have a good, game colt, ready to run the race of his career," said Max Hirsch, the trainer of Tick On. "He is a bit uncertain at the post, but with any kind of racing luck I look for him to be returned the winner. I will have no alibi."

Tick On's credentials were anything but impressive. The fact that he, as the favorite, had lost six races in a row and had an overall record of just three triumphs in eleven starts underlined the poor caliber of this Derby field. "Several of the field were potential or actual selling players, placed in the race either because their wealthy owners wished to see their colors in the Derby, or because their not so wealthy owners had come to the conclusion it was such an open race that anything might win it," stated *The Blood-Horse* magazine. "The field was the poorest in quality that has contested a Derby for several years."

Norris Royden of the *New York Daily Running Horse* said the field "probably was the worst from a point of class" since 1925. Of the twenty starters, only four—Adobe Post, Brother Joe, Hoops, and Lucky Tom—were coming into the race off a victory. Somebody had to be favored, though, and that honor went to Tick On.

H. J. ("Derby Dick") Thompson, trainer of the Bradley entry, had respect for Tick On. "Burgoo King is ready,"

Owner Col. E. R. Bradley (left) and trainer H. J. ("Derby Dick") Thompson teamed to win four runnings of the Kentucky Derby: 1921 with Behave Yourself, 1926 with Bubbling Over, 1932 with Burgoo King, and 1933 with Brokers Tip. (Photo courtesy Keeneland-Cook)

Thompson said. "If we can beat Max, we are going to keep the honors here in Kentucky. Brother Joe's chances would be enhanced in the event of a muddy track."

Bradley feared only Tick On. "I will not be disappointed if Tick On should win," declared Bradley, "but I shall be very much disappointed if any other mount beats my entry. My horses are fit and ready to go the distance. They will go to the post with no excuse to offer as to the outcome, and I don't believe they will need one."

Tick On, owned by the Loma Stable, also was liked by many newsmen. He was picked to win by Buck Weaver and Louis McNeely of *The Louisville Times,* Harvey Woodruff of the *Chicago Tribune,* and Alan Gould of the Associated Press, as well as Damon Runyon. The widely read Bert E. Collyer went with the Mrs. John H. Whitney entry of Stepenfetchit and Over Time. The entry was ridden by two veterans making comebacks, Ensor on Stepenfetchit and Sande on Over Time.

Accounts differed as to which horse, Burgoo King or Brother Joe, was considered superior by the Bradley stable. Brother Joe didn't have much of a racing record, but he had the breeding. He was closely related to Blue Larkspur, the 1929 champion three-year-old who raced for Bradley. Both had the same dam, Blossom Time. Brother Joe was by Black Toney, the father of Blue Larkspur's sire, Black Servant.

Olin Gentry, a longtime Bradley employee, once recalled that Brother Joe earlier was considered superior to Burgoo King but that the stable changed its opinion as the Derby neared. "Brother Joe went into winter quarters as the best prospect because he could run and he was a brother to Blue Larkspur," said Gentry. "But Brother Joe went lame. He had a bad leg. I think he went in there with a half-bowed tendon. I don't know why in the hell they ran him. But anyhow we just thought Burgoo King was the best before the Derby 'cause the other horse wasn't sound."

Certain news accounts leading up to the Derby indicated that the Bradley camp leaned toward Burgoo King over Brother Joe. *The Louisville Times* reported that three days before the Derby the Bradley "stable connections finally declared themselves as favoring Burgoo King, but let it be known that chief reliance would be placed in Brother Joe in the event of a muddy track."

Further, when Bradley learned during Derby Week that a Louisville sportswriter had made a meager future-book bet on Brother Joe, the owner said, "Shame it couldn't have been on Burgoo King." (James T. Looney, the man for whom Burgoo King was named, had his money on the right horse. Looney wagered fifty dollars at odds of 40-1 on Burgoo King in the Derby's future book.)

Yet another story indicated that the Derby loss didn't detract from Bradley's opinion of Brother Joe. After the colt was injured in the Derby and finished ahead of only a horse that had broken down, *The Courier-Journal* reported, "Mr. Bradley contended all along that Brother Joe was the better colt of the two and he has not weakened on him yet, as his race in the Derby does not count."

Burgoo King had only one three-year-old race before the Derby. He finished second, beaten three lengths by Brother Joe in the Dixiana Purse at Lexington. Burgoo King was ridden by his regular jockey, Fator. It was Burgoo King's thirteenth race, and the twelfth time that Fator had been aboard him.

Brother Joe, winless in two starts in 1931, was ridden for the first time by Fator in his three-year-old debut, a second-place finish at Lexington. Just three days later, on April 22, Brother Joe had James in the saddle for his victory over Burgoo King in the Dixiana Purse. Brother Joe thus didn't break his maiden until fifteen days before the Derby.

History is unclear as to why Fator wound up riding Brother Joe instead of Burgoo King. Fator, the stable's first-string jockey, originally was expected to ride Burgoo King.

However, according to one story, he was assigned the mount on Brother Joe because that colt was considered the harder of the two Bradley horses to handle.

Another reporter noted, "Original plans were to give Fator his pick, which would have been Burgoo King on the fast and Brother Joe in the mud, but at the last minute it was decided to entrust him with the reins of Brother Joe. Burgoo King always has been a rapid beginner and it was thought that Fator's experience might come in good stead on the slower-breaking Brother Joe." Still another story claimed that Fator gave up the Derby mount because of superstition. When Burgoo King drew the number-thirteen post position, Fator was said to have shifted to Brother Joe.

James, a former newsboy who delivered papers on a route near his home a short distance from Churchill Downs, had ridden in one previous Derby, finishing last aboard Prince d'Amour in 1931.

At the time of entry, Bradley's stable agent, Moss Cossman, instructed, "Leave the jockeys blank until tomorrow."

On the day of the race, readers of *The Louisville Times* might have been a bit confused. On page 1, the lineup of Derby starters listed Fator on Brother Joe and James on Burgoo King. Yet back in the sports section, it was reported on one page that Fator was hoping to win the Derby with Burgoo King, and on another page the jockey was pictured on the colt. The cutlines stated that he had the mount on Burgoo King in the $50,000-added race.

The Courier-Journal and *The New York Times,* in their issues on Derby Day, also listed Fator on Burgoo King and James on Brother Joe. "Burgoo King is rated the better of the two on a dry track and will have Laverne Fator in the saddle, with Eugene James up on Brother Joe," wrote Bryan Field in *The New York Times.* "If rain comes, Brother Joe is deemed more formidable, and Fator will shift mounts with James."

The rain didn't come, but Fator shifted mounts anyway. As

great as Fator was, he never won a Triple Crown race. He was 0 for 4 in the Derby, 0 for 3 in the Preakness, and 0 for 4 in the Belmont. This Derby was his last Triple Crown mount.

The Derby was the first stakes victory for Burgoo King. A son of 1926 Derby winner Bubbling Over, Burgoo King had raced in seven previous stakes, each in 1931. He finished ninth in the Sanford, fourteenth in the Hopeful, fourth in the Champagne, ninth in the Futurity at Belmont Park, fifth in the Richard Johnson Stakes, seventh in the Spalding Lowe Jenkins Handicap, and third in the Pimlico Futurity.

In a dozen starts at two, he had four victories, one in a maiden race and three in allowances, with earnings of $6,000. His defeat in his lone 1932 Derby prep race dropped his record to nine losses in thirteen starts. He and Brother Joe went off as the third choice in the betting.

A crowd estimated from thirty-five to fifty thousand turned out for the Derby, the classic's smallest gathering in some years. Heavyweight boxing champion Max Schmeling was among the celebrities. He liked Stepenfetchit's chances.

About five thousand swarming fans, disregarding mounted patrolmen and other security men, charged into the infield without paying. Some crashed through the gates while others climbed over, or cut their way through, a wire fence taller than nine feet. The wave of humanity didn't stop in the infield. As was customary in those days, many fans invaded the clubhouse and grandstand, which were far from being filled. The onslaught got out of hand, and policemen finally could do no more than lean against the rail and wave disapprovingly at the men and boys streaming across the track throughout the day.

Men wearing corduroys, overalls, and sweatshirts, as well as some who went shirtless, rubbed elbows in the clubhouse with high society. Hobos and college students mingled with the wealthy. Obviously, those patrons who had purchased box seats were incensed over the intrusion. "In some instances boxholders upon going to the shed to place wagers returned to find their chairs gone and uninvited guests selling them at $1 apiece on the lawn," reported *The Louisville Times*.

In view of the warm weather, enterprising youths filled pop bottles with water from infield hydrants and sold the cool drinks to the crowd. The water went for ten cents a bottle.

Money was scarce in those days, and betting for the seven races totaled $850,809, lowest since 1919. The wagering would have been greater "had the commission on the betting been 5 per cent, as formerly, instead of 10 per cent, as now," *The Blood-Horse* magazine opined. "The depression, of course, had some effect on the decrease in the total turnover, but it did not, we think, have as much to do with the decline as did the increased commission."

Just before the Derby, the crowd's attention was caught by two army observation planes undertaking practice maneuvers over the Downs. "The two ships, about 5,000 feet up, zoomed and cruised slowly about like two lazy dragonflies hovering in mid-air," reported *The Thoroughbred Record* magazine.

Prior to the post parade there was another parade on the track. The Louisville American Legion fife and drum corps, in flashy red-and-white uniforms, marched up and down the homestretch. During the noisy program, certain Derby horses were on their way to the paddock, and they reared and shied from the blasts of the trumpeters. Tick On later gave starter William Hamilton all kinds of trouble at the barrier, and the colt's supporters believed that he had been upset badly by all the hoopla.

Tick On was the chief culprit at the post, but Cee Tee, Prince Hotspur, Cathop, Cold Check, and Our Fancy also acted up. Burgoo King, meanwhile, was on his best behavior.

With the field probably causing more problems at the barrier than any other in Derby history, the break was delayed 15½ or 16 minutes before Hamilton finally let 'em go.

The race wasn't particularly exciting. Burgoo King ran close to the pace, overtook Economic in the upper stretch, and won easily, by five lengths. Economic, a 16-1 shot, finished second. Tick On, shut off in the first couple of strides, was caught in the middle of a bumping-and-crowding traffic jam on the clubhouse turn, and his rider, Walls, had trouble maintaining his seat. Tick On came in sixth.

Brother Joe was eased near the end by Fator. This bad-legged colt couldn't have beaten Broadway Joe, bad knees and all, in the Derby. By the time he crossed the wire, Brother Joe was nineteenth, some forty-five lengths behind Burgoo King.

The track was officially rated fast by *Daily Racing Form,* although it was listed as good by another publication. Burgoo King's time of 2:05⅕ was far off the track record of 2:01⅘ set by Twenty Grand the previous year. Burgoo King no doubt could have run faster—he did only what he had to do to win—but the fact remains that no official fast-track Derby since then has had a slower clocking.

At the finish of the Derby, one radio announcer told his audience that Burgoo King had been ridden by Mack Garner. Actually, Garner was aboard Liberty Limited, who failed even to finish.

James, whose contract was purchased by Bradley from the estate of Joseph Leiter a short time before the Derby, was interviewed afterward by a movie outfit. A movie man asked the jockey to say merely that he was Eugene James, winner of the Kentucky Derby. Instead, the rider elaborated a bit, stating, "I'm Eugene James, who rode Col. E. R. Bradley's Burgoo King to win the Kentucky Derby. Colonel Bradley bought my contract from the Leiter estate, and I certainly am glad to have won for him."

While the Bradley stable was celebrating its victory, pretty Mary Hirsch was crying. She was the daughter of Max Hirsch, the trainer of Tick On, and the young woman watched the race from her dappled pony in the infield, waiting to take the colt to the winner's circle. But a not-so-funny thing happened to Tick On in the Derby. He lost. Tears flowed freely from the heartbroken Miss Hirsch's eyes as she saw Tick On cross the finish line, beaten almost six lengths.

But at least he crossed the wire. Liberty Limited, making his first start of the year, broke down and didn't finish. Brother Joe, whose troublesome leg began to bother him going down the backstretch, was gimpy afterward and subsequently was turned out at Bradley's farm. Liberty Limited and Brother Joe were incapacitated for the rest of 1932.

Other Derby casualties were Gallant Sir, whose shoulder was kicked and bruised at the post; Brandon Mint, who was cut about his ankles and lost much blood; and Prince Hotspur, bothered by a severely bruised stifle. Prince Hotspur, viciously kicked twice at the barrier, appeared to pull up in good shape, and the effects of the blows weren't noticed until later.

Two of those casualties failed to win after running in the Derby—Brandon Mint, who went 0 for 12, and Liberty Limited, 0 for 1. Lucky Tom (0 for 5) was another starter who didn't win afterward.

From the Derby, Burgoo King went on to win the Preakness the following week, edging Tick On by a head. Two weeks later, Burgoo King finished next-to-last in the Withers, a race run on a sloppy track. "Burgoo King sprawled in the going," declared the chart's footnotes in *Daily Racing Form.*

He then bowed a tendon while training, a problem that probably traced back to the Withers. He didn't start again for almost two years and was trained to a sulky while preparing for his comeback.

Burgoo King resumed his career at Churchill Downs on May 7, 1934, the two-year anniversary of his Derby victory. He ran second and was sent to New York. He had four starts in the Big Apple, each time with Meade riding him. Burgoo

King finished third in a mile allowance, then scored a 1½-length victory at that distance in another allowance. He followed up with another triumph, this time by 2 lengths. In the last race of his career, he was sent off as the Queens County Handicap's 3-5 favorite but finished third, beating one horse.

Burgoo King retired with a record of eight victories, two seconds, and three thirds in twenty-one starts with earnings of $110,940. Almost half of his money total—$52,350—came from winning the Derby. Burgoo King was the third of four Derby winners owned by Bradley. He was the only one to win after the Derby.

The 1932 Derby field was forgotten in a hurry. The twenty members of the cast earned $617,426 from a total of 1,128 races, an average of $547 per start. Just two—Burgoo King and Gallant Sir (sixteen of forty-two)—won more than one-third of their races. Only Stepenfetchit, Tick On, Gallant Sir, and Crystal Prince won stakes after their three-year-old seasons.

Five horses from that crop who didn't run in the Derby—the champion triumvirate of Top Flight ($275,900), Burning Blaze ($84,325), and Faireno ($182,215), as well as Gusto ($151,655) and Universe ($33,425)—earned a total of $727,520 in career purses, $110,094 more than all twenty Derby starters. Furthermore, these five stars earned their money in one-sixth the number of starts—179.

It could have been quite a spectacle, the 1932 Derby. As it was, the race and its aftermath stamped this renewal as nothing more than the Depression Derby.

17

Black Gold:
The King of Derby Winners

HE WAS THE KING of Derby winners. In 1924, he won the Louisiana Derby and later the Kentucky Derby, two of four derbies that he captured that season. He achieved turf immortality, and in 1989 he was enshrined in racing's Hall of Fame in Saratoga Springs, New York.

Meet Black Gold, whose story is one of the most fascinating and poignant in the history of Thoroughbred racing. The tale of how he came to be bred, how he reached turf stardom, and how he came to a tragic death is packed with drama. Join us as we turn back the clock and relive the Black Gold story.

Whether he ran off a groom with a rifle, slipped away like a thief in the night, or simply intimidated the stewards, Al Hoots had no intention of giving up Useeit to anybody. Such was Hoots' attachment to his mare. And such was the beginning of a story that led to Louisiana Derby and Kentucky Derby victories for a son of Useeit.

Hoots didn't live to see Black Gold sweep to his four derby victories in 1924, but his wife, Rosa, was on hand to watch the little black colt, known as "the Indian horse," win the fiftieth running of the Kentucky Derby.

The Black Gold story has spun off more legends than any other in racing history. Separating fact from fiction is sometimes impossible in connection with the events surrounding this horse. His story had it all—a sentimental owner who didn't live to see his dream fulfilled, a colt whose victory in the Kentucky Derby actually ran bookies out of business, and a sad ending. The Black Gold tale, in short, was perfect stuff for Hollywood. Indeed, a movie was made about him, but unfortunately it was like virtually everything Hollywood has ever done on horse racing—bad.

The story starts with Al and Rosa Hoots, who were married in 1886. Mrs. Hoots, whose parents were pioneers in the West, was born near Independence, Kansas, in 1869. Her father was active in Osage Indian tribal affairs and often acted as an interpreter in their dealings with white men. Her mother, Aunt Jane, was said to have owned more than ten thousand head of cattle at one time and was known as the "Cattle Queen of the Osages." One story said of her, "Not only was she a cattlewoman, but she was a good horsewoman and a crack shot with the pistol. She has many romantic experiences; many trials and tribulations; but she always had the kind heart that tempered many a storm."

As for Useeit's heritage, she was a brown filly by Bonnie Joe—Effie M., by Bowling Green. She was bred by C. B. Campbell, a rich rancher, thirteen miles north of Chickasha, Oklahoma, on what was once Indian territory. Campbell named her Useeit because a water cooler in his bank had that brand name on the water bottle.

Useeit made her career debut at Tulsa on October 21, 1909, and finished last in a field of six going 4½ furlongs. Two races and five days later, she broke her maiden, winning a 4½-furlong allowance by three lengths at Tulsa. Useeit won that race for the partnership of Riddle & Louthon.

History is unclear whether Hoots later bought the tiny brown filly from John Riddle or Millard Halcomb. Hoots, a cattleman and horse raiser, traded eighty acres of land near Skiatook, Oklahoma, for the filly in 1910 or 1911.

Hoots, who previously had raced some cheap horses, ran Useeit in Tulsa, Oklahoma City, and Muskogee for two or three years, and she became a local favorite. She raced in match races, at dusty county fairs, and in bullrings.

Hoots' health then began to suffer, and he was advised that the climate in Canada might help him. Therefore, in 1913, he and his wife packed up and headed there. And Useeit went along. Hoots intended to race her at the big tracks, an idea that more than a few racing people thought was foolish for this "bush" mare. Others, however, believed—as Hoots did—that Useeit had the ability to more than hold her own against such opposition, and she did just that.

She raced all over in a career that finally ended in Juarez, Mexico, on February 22, 1916. On that day, Hoots entered her in a selling race, a predecessor to the modern-day claiming races. It's unknown why Hoots would have risked Useeit by putting her in a such a race, unless he didn't know she was in an actual selling race, didn't understand the racing rules pertaining to selling races, or perhaps thought he had a gentlemen's agreement among horsemen that nobody would take her from him. Either that or, according to one story, Hoots "said his partner in the particular enterprise had tricked him into entering the mare in the race with the promise" that she wouldn't be taken from him.

Whether it was a deception, misunderstanding, or something else, Useeit was eligible to be bought, which is exactly what happened. A horseman by the name of Tobe Ramsey purchased her out of the race for a price variously reported as $500 or $600. Rather, Ramsey *thought* he bought her. Take your pick as to what happened next.

Story one: Following the race, a groom for Ramsey came by Hoots' barn to pick up Useeit. To the groom's surprise, Hoots grabbed a rifle from his tack room. Not sticking around to ask questions, the groom departed in a hurry . . . and so did Hoots, who hastened to the railroad yard with Useeit and took her to Oklahoma.

Story two: Following the race, Hoots arrived on the scene

to take Useeit back to his barn. Col. Matt Winn of Churchill
Downs said in his book, *Down the Stretch:*

> He was told she had been sold. He seemed bewil-
> dered; refused to believe it. The rules were explained.
> They didn't make sense to him, but he agreed that he
> would turn over the horse the next day, if permitted to
> take her back to his barn so he could say good-by to
> her. The consent was given. Sometime during the
> night, Hoots and Useeit quit Mexico. He took his be-
> loved mare back across the border, someway, some-
> how, and she was routed to his Oklahoma home.

Story three: Once Hoots grabbed his rifle and showed that
he meant business, the Mexican racing officials decided to
keep peace instead of doing anything to cause this stubborn
horseman to pull the trigger. Therefore, the stewards officially allowed Hoots to keep Useeit.

But even though he kept the horse, Hoots was finished in
the racing game. Because Hoots violated racing rules by not
giving up his horse to Ramsey, Hoots and Useeit both were
ruled off the turf for life, a fate the sentimental owner preferred rather than lose his horse. Useeit completed her
lengthy career with thirty or thirty-four victories in 119 or
122 starts.

Accounts differ as to whether the Hoots family was now
living in Oklahoma or Kentucky, but most seem to agree
that Al took his horse home in a boxcar to Oklahoma. It is
said that Col. E. R. Bradley, the influential Kentucky horseman and gambler, helped get Useeit reinstated on Hoots'
behalf for breeding purposes. With that accomplished,
Hoots looked forward to the day when he could breed
Useeit to a fine stallion, a mating that he dreamed would
produce a Derby winner. Bradley, it was said, had been impressed with Useeit's speed and offered Hoots a breeding
season to his fashionable stallion, Black Toney.

Hoots died the next year in Eureka Springs, Arkansas,
and, according to legend, while on his deathbed he made

Rosa promise to keep Useeit and breed her someday to Black Toney. That mating eventually did take place several years later, and when the foal was born on February 17, 1921, Mrs. Hoots picked a natural name for the youngster, a strapping coal-black colt with a faint fleck of white between his eyes. "I named him after the 'Black Gold' oil in Oklahoma. That's what they call it," said Mrs. Hoots.

Mrs. Hoots didn't see Black Gold until he was a two-year-old. The colt was raised by his trainer, Hanley Webb, a rugged horseman who didn't waste much time after the colt turned two before putting him into competition. On January 8, 1923, Black Gold and six other juveniles came out for their career debuts in a three-furlong sprint at the Fair Grounds track in New Orleans. Sent off as the 6-5 favorite, Useeit's colt justified the bettors' faith in him by hitting the finish line six lengths on top. Black Gold thus had started his career at the Fair Grounds . . . and he would end it there five years later.

The colt's legend began to take shape following this race, with J. E. Crown writing in the *New Orleans States* on February 25, 1923:

> Before he died, old man Hoots whispered in Useeit's ear: "You will go back to the races. A son of yours will perpetuate the name of the gamest pony that ever looked through a bridle, and I will ride him and I will look after him; I will pet him as I have petted you. The love that I have given you will send him to the races and everybody will say: 'Useeit has sent a champion back to the turf.'"

The following month, Mrs. Hoots was offered $25,000 for Black Gold, but she had no intention of parting with her colt.

The colt won nine of his eighteen starts as a two-year-old and then reeled off victories in his first four races of 1924 before the Kentucky Derby. He had won the four races, including the Louisiana Derby, by a total of eighteen or nineteen lengths. His impressive past performances, coupled with the fact that three prominent three-year-olds—Sazaren, Wise Counsellor, and St. James—were destined to miss the Kentucky Derby, would establish him as the post-time favorite for the Churchill Downs classic.

Black Gold had been anything but a favorite in the winter book earlier in the year, some bookies offering odds as high as 100-1 on the colt. As betting support started to show on him, his odds gradually dropped from 50-1 to 20-1 to 10-1 and then 8-1. The bookies weren't particularly concerned about Black Gold because he was still overshadowed by the Big Three. However, Sazaren, Wise Counsellor, and St. James became no-shows for the Derby, and Useeit's colt inherited the role as favorite.

Following Black Gold's victory in the Derby Trial at Churchill Downs, one bettor made a large wager on the colt in Louisville but couldn't get higher than 4-1. Meanwhile, in New Orleans, the price dropped all the way down to 3-1 on Black Gold.

Mrs. Hoots, convinced her colt would win the Derby, even brought a box of cigars to Churchill Downs to present to Colonel Winn after the race. Black Gold lived up to Mrs. Hoots' expectations, providing a romantic touch to the Kentucky Derby by winning by a half-length in an exciting finish.

After the Derby, certain readers of *The Courier-Journal* in Louisville might have needed handkerchiefs to wipe their eyes after digesting a story by one John Francis. Francis wrote that Al Hoots, not long after returning to Oklahoma with Useeit,

> became ill and just before his death he called Mrs. Hoots to his bedside. Seeing, perhaps, with the half-delirious clearness of those about to pass into a world where, tradition has it, vision is multiplied untold times, Hoots poured into ears which listened with affectionate interest, the story of his love for Useeit, the little mare.

He told of his painstaking efforts with the little mare; the qualities which made her a commendable racer; her quickness at the barrier and an understanding unknown to most horses. After extolling the virtues of this little mare, he told Mrs. Hoots, with failing breaths, to breed the mare to a stallion of proven worth.

"My spirit always will be with the foal of this mare," he told her. "The foal will be possessed of the wings of a tornado and the fire which is known only to the plains horses, which have so often proven their willingness to give their last tiny bit of strength for their riders," he said. "Plains horses are known for their courage," he continued, "and I see this foal, possessed of the undaunted spirit of a mother descended from horses which admitted defeat only in death, surprising the racing world."

Winning the Kentucky Derby thrust Webb into racing's spotlight, a place where the fifty-four-year-old trainer was unaccustomed to being. Webb, a native of Pattonsburg, Missouri, punched cattle as a cowboy for fifteen years in Indian territory and then worked as a U.S. marshal for ten years. He had been around horses on the plains for a number of years but had never trained them until 1913, when he went to work for the Hoots family.

Webb, a hard-drinking man, asked a lot of his horses, and now with Black Gold, he was the target of much criticism. Make no mistake about it, second guessing trainers has long been a racetrack tradition, but in the case of Webb, his methods with this colt came in for particular reproach, and he was ridiculed by more than a few horsemen. In retrospect, Webb obviously was in over his head training a horse of Black Gold's ability. Yet, in the immediate afterglow of the fiftieth Kentucky Derby, the trainer was praised in certain corners. *The Thoroughbred Record* magazine, in its account, called Webb "a good trainer" and said he "must be given credit with knowing how to thoroughly prepare a horse for a great race and how to keep the horse at the top of his form throughout the racing season."

Black Gold's triumph was anything but popular with bookmakers. For years, the 1924 Derby was remembered as "The Great Runout" or "Black Saturday" for bookies throughout the country. Indeed, when Black Gold stopped running in the Derby, some bookmakers started.

"Winter books were big then," longtime Derby observer Mike Barry once recalled. "There were a lot of winter-book bookmakers in Louisville, and they were all over the country. These bookmakers had all laid good prices on Black Gold, and they just took a terrible bath. A lot of them just left town, couldn't pay off."

A week after the Kentucky Derby, Black Gold was back in action, running in the 1⅛-mile Ohio State Derby. Mrs. Hoots wasn't on hand to watch the race, but she didn't miss much of a contest. It was strictly a breeze for Black Gold, who won as he pleased, crossing the finish line eight lengths on top.

The colt later won the Chicago Derby at Hawthorne, carrying high weight of 129 pounds to a six-length victory. That was his fourth derby victory of the year, the other three coming in the Louisiana Derby, Kentucky Derby, and Ohio State Derby. Black Gold wound up the year with a record of nine victories in thirteen starts and earnings of $91,340.

It appeared for a while that he might return to competition in 1925, but this colt, who was no stranger to soreness, failed to stand training and didn't make it back to the races. He was retired to stud, going to stand at Jack Howard's Rookwood Farm, near Lexington, Kentucky. His stud fee was listed as "$500 cash at time of service."

Black Gold, however, was sterile, although he did sire one foal, who was killed by lightning. Even though he now had no future at stud, Black Gold should have stayed at Rookwood or some other farm for the rest of his life. He wouldn't have it so good, though.

Instead of allowing Black Gold to spend his time grazing and romping around a pasture in a life of leisure, the decision was made to bring him back to the races. Past his prime, he had been away from competition for too long and had never been the soundest horse in the world in the first place. Even so, Black Gold was returned to training.

The stable's plan was to point the colt for the 1928 New Orleans Handicap. Webb wrote J.D. Mooney a letter, hoping the jockey would ride Black Gold in his comeback. Mooney checked with his brother, Joe, who was riding in New Orleans at the time. Joe informed J.D. that Black Gold was lame. Handling the situation diplomatically so as not to hurt Webb's feelings, J.D. wrote that his Canadian owner wouldn't permit him to go to New Orleans to ride. But Mooney didn't want Black Gold to be injured. "I asked them not to run him," he recalled.

Webb didn't heed the jockey's advice, and on December 17, 1927, Black Gold returned to the races after being away from competition for more than three years. He ran with stablemate and full brother Beggar Boy in a 5½-furlong allowance at Jefferson Park in New Orleans. Beggar Boy, a three-year-old colt, won by a nose to bring home $700 of the $1,000 purse. Black Gold failed to earn a dime, finishing fifth under top weight of 117 pounds.

Six days later, carrying high weight of 114 pounds, Black Gold ran fourth in a one-mile allowance, the Mississippi Purse, and earned his last paycheck—fifty dollars. The old horse couldn't talk, but the footnotes in the *Daily Racing Form*'s chart came through with a message that was loud and clear: "Black Gold raced forwardly for three-quarters, then tired and finished lame." If only Hanley Webb had been aware.

Webb came back just three days later and started this six-year-old cripple in the 1¹⁄₁₆-mile Christmas Handicap. Black Gold dragged himself home in ninth place under top weight of 120 pounds, again finishing lame. Still, Webb didn't pick up on—or chose to ignore—these obvious signs.

Three starts, and Black Gold finished all out of the money. He was hardly a shadow of his onetime greatness, and it was degrading for him to have to continue to perform at a level so far below the capabilities of his heyday. His fans certainly didn't want to see him running, not *this* Black Gold.

Many racetrackers shook their heads, unable to believe what was being done to the horse. As one old-timer recalled many years ago, "Clockers and horsemen felt sorry for the old horse. He was as sore as a boil all over, and his legs were very weak. They knew he had no chance. Every time he worked he'd hobble back to the barn. He ran a few times at Jefferson Park, and he came back lame after each race. It's a wonder to me that the stewards didn't refuse further entry of the horse."

On January 18, 1928, Black Gold ran for the last time. He appeared in the one-mile Salome Purse, a $1,200 race that was the supporting feature on the Fair Grounds program. On the day of the race, *The New Orleans Item* carried a run-down on the Fair Grounds races and next to Black Gold's name came this remark: "Webb thinks he can do it." *The Times-Picayune,* on the other hand, didn't keep Black Gold's unsoundness a secret. "Black Gold has worked well but his bad leg makes it look hopeless for him," the newspaper said for all the world to read.

And, yet, he ran anyway. He ran as fast and as far as he could. Carrying high weight of 115 pounds and sent off as the fifth choice at 8.18-1 odds, he broke from the number-one post position, the same slot he had started from in the '24 Kentucky Derby, and he demonstrated a good early lick of speed. Reaching out for all he was worth, he gave his backers hope as the horses raced down the backstretch and rounded the far turn. And as the field straightened out for home, he kept digging in, kept giving it his best, and was still in contention, battling it out for second place on the inside.

And then it happened. With a sixteenth of a mile to go, he stumbled and nearly fell. Apprentice jockey Dave Emery raised up and attempted to stop Black Gold. The horse's left foreleg had snapped just above the ankle.

The injury occurred in full view of the spectators, many of whom gasped at the pitiful sight of Black Gold, on three legs now, struggling toward the finish. He was in the heat of competition, with the adrenaline flowing at a high level, and he continued doing what he, as a noble Thoroughbred, was born to do. He kept on running, giving every last ounce of energy in his body in an attempt to reach the wire.

Black Gold was pulled up by Emery right in front of the stands. Many in the crowd couldn't bear to look at the horse, whose hoof was hanging on by what amounted to no more than a thread. Emery quickly dismounted.

Black Gold, on the ground and in tremendous pain, futilely tried to get to his feet. It was 4:05 P.M. Black Gold had only a short time left to live. "He was led back of the paddock, and still shaking his proud and perfect head in resentment at the tight hold taken on him by an assistant, he flinched as the needle of destruction pricked his skin, tossed his head high and pricked his ears even as the needle was withdrawn and the next fraction of a second dropped dead," reported *The Times-Picayune*.

Black Gold was buried the next day in the track's infield beside the grave of Pan Zareta, the "Queen of the Turf" and another Fair Grounds favorite who had died of pneumonia in New Orleans ten years earlier. A top sprinter during her racing days, Pan Zareta had competed against Black Gold's mother, Useeit. Following his burial, *The Times-Picayune* reported:

> Black Gold's death has plunged the racing colony here in mourning. It will be many a long day before the feats of the little wonder horse will be forgotten by

racegoers; certainly Orleanians long will have reason to remember him, as his grave in the Fair Grounds infield will be a reminder.

Black Gold was buried yesterday and his interment found tears flooding the eyes of many a hardened race track veteran. Hanley Webb, who loved every hair in Black Gold's hide, was as a man who has lost his best friend.

Of course, Webb is being severely criticized for going on with Black Gold in the face of lameness which developed in both his two races previous to the fatal one. But then, Black Gold was the apple of Webb's eye; he had boasted that Black Gold was going to come back and he wanted to see the little fellow make good.

Webb had raised Black Gold, and now he was with the horse at the end. "I am responsible for his death," he said. "I never paid any attention to his lameness. He always seemed to work out of it. As God is my witness, I ran him in good faith."

The legend of Black Gold (1921-28) will never die.

18

Seattle Slew
Was a Special Racehorse

I WILL ALWAYS HAVE a special place in my heart for Seattle Slew, that brilliant runner who swept the Kentucky Derby, Preakness, and Belmont in 1977. He remains the only horse ever to win the Triple Crown with an unbeaten record. Seattle Slew had speed, talent, and, most of all, courage. Those of us who saw him race and recognized his ability at an early age will always be grateful that he came along to show us that the great ones don't need excuses. They just go out there and do their jobs.

By Bold Reasoning out of My Charmer, this colt was bred by Ben S. Castleman and was foaled on his White Horse Acres in Lexington. He sold for $17,500 at the 1975 Fasig-Tipton Company of Kentucky's summer yearling sale. As a two- and three-year-old, he was owned by Mickey and Karen Taylor, a couple from White Swan, Washington, and Dr. Jim Hill, a veterinarian, and his wife, Sally.

In 1976, Seattle Slew won all three of his starts, including a 9¾-length romp in the Champagne, and was voted champion two-year-old colt.

He embarked on his three-year-old season with Jean Cruguet riding him to a track-record victory in a seven-furlong allowance at Hialeah Park (1:20⅗). "Cruguet eased him the last sixteenth, and he still broke the track record—it's unbelievable," said Billy Turner, the trainer of Seattle Slew.

The colt came into the 1977 Kentucky Derby with a six-for-six record. On the way over from the stable area, Mickey Taylor was leading Seattle Slew on one side; groom John Polston was on the other. "When he was right in front [of the stand], they started 'The Star-Spangled Banner' with the cymbals and he went sky high," Mickey recalled in an interview in late 1996. "The only people who probably jumped any higher than him were John and me trying to hold him on the ground."

As the horses walked through the tunnel leading to the paddock, they had their lip tattoos checked by the identifier. It was no secret that this was Seattle Slew, the heavy favorite for the Kentucky Derby, being led to the paddock, but the identifier, who was just doing his job, made the mistake of attempting to lift up this fiery colt's lip. "When he went through the tunnel, he was really prancing, and the guy tried lifting up his lip," Taylor said. "We had told him, 'You can't do it.' Just like you can't tie his tongue. He wasn't mean, but he just wouldn't let you do it. And he walked right over the guy who was lifting up the lip. From then on, he was pretty well on his toes."

In 1977, the Downs had a cramped paddock, and horses sometimes would become upset in the crowded conditions. Such was the case with the high-strung Seattle Slew. "He was just dripping wet," Taylor recalled. "He wasn't shaking. It was just like you took a hose and washed him down in the paddock."

Taylor thought the colt's temperament and the humidity in the paddock led to Seattle Slew's heavy sweating. "I remember people trying to shake my hand, and I looked underneath him, and the bark in his stall was absolutely brown from water. I don't know how much weight he lost in that paddock. He wasn't shaking; he wasn't nervous; his eye was alert."

Seattle Slew was the 1-2 favorite, and the only way he figured to lose the race was for him to get locked into the starting gate. That didn't happen, but he got off to a nearly disastrous start, veering to the right as he came out of the gate from his number-four post position. After slightly losing his balance in the saddle, Cruguet then began the work of getting Seattle Slew back into the Derby.

"I had to make a decision, and I decided to go," the jockey recalled. "I didn't want to be behind a bunch of horses. If I sit still, I'm going to be behind ten or twelve horses on the first turn and that'd be the end of me. I kinda bulled my way through between two horses to get me where I wanted to be on the first turn."

Seattle Slew charged through the field so rapidly that by the first time he reached the wire he was battling For The Moment for the lead. He eventually put away For The Moment and then held off the stretch runners. In a brilliant performance, Seattle Slew won by a length and three-quarters. From the quarter pole to the wire, Cruguet whipped the colt eleven times.

"Seattle Slew was the most deserving winner in the history of the Derby," declared the late Louisville newspaperman Mike Barry, who saw all but four runnings of the Churchill Downs classic from 1922 through 1991. "In all the Derbies I've seen, I never saw a horse have as much trouble as Seattle Slew had and still win the race. He was really a good horse."

Others praised Seattle Slew for his remarkable race. Mickey Taylor said that probably the greatest compliment he and Karen ever received on Seattle Slew came from E. P. Taylor, the owner-breeder of 1964 Kentucky Derby winner Northern Dancer. This Canadian horseman came up to the Taylors and Turner after the 1977 Derby and said, "This horse will make a tremendous sire because of the way he made it through the paddock and the way he ran."

Looking back on that remark, Mickey said, "I thought that was a hell of a compliment coming from a man like him."

Seattle Slew next captured the Preakness. With a record Preakness crowd of 77,346 looking on at historic Pimlico, Seattle Slew ran extremely fast early and still had enough in reserve to win by a length and a half over Iron Constitution. Confidently ridden by Cruguet, Seattle Slew was timed in 1:54⅖ for the mile and three-sixteenths, just two-fifths of a second off Canonero II's official record for the Preakness. "The horse met the challenge today," said Turner, who expertly trained Seattle Slew through the Triple Crown series. "It was a fast race—what I call one of his best performances."

The next stop was the Belmont Stakes. "I don't think he can lose," Cruguet said before the race. "The only thing that can beat him is the last quarter of a mile. That's a question to this point because nobody knows. But I think he can go a mile and a half. Bold Forbes was a sprinter, and he won the Belmont last year. If he won at a mile and a half, I think I can, too. No question about that. I think he'll win this race much easier than the Derby and Preakness. He'll win with more power."

The Belmont wasn't Seattle Slew's best distance. "He was a top mile horse," Cruguet said years later. "He was not a mile-and-a-half horse." Even so, he led throughout the Belmont to triumph by four lengths.

"This was the easiest race in the Triple Crown," Mickey Taylor said afterward, holding a glass of champagne as he and others in his party toasted Seattle Slew's victory. "He didn't have to extend himself. Jean's done a fantastic job with him."

A vacation clearly was needed for Seattle Slew, but instead he was sent to California in an ill-advised trip and he suffered his first defeat, finishing fourth as the 1-5 favorite in the Swaps Stakes on July 3. He obviously wasn't himself and trailed by sixteen lengths at the wire. For one reason or another, he didn't race again in 1977, but his Triple Crown sweep earned him the Horse of the Year title.

While in Florida in early 1978, Seattle Slew suffered a

near-fatal illness, developing an infection and a fever that climbed dangerously high. For several days and nights, his life appeared to be in danger, but he came around slowly.

In late February, it was announced that the Taylors and the Hills had sold a half-interest in Seattle Slew to George A. ("Joe") Layman, Jr. (25 percent) of Yakima, Washington; Franklin Groves (12.5 percent) of Minneapolis; and Spendthrift Farm's Brownell Combs (12.5 percent). With a price of $6 million for twenty of the forty shares in the syndicate, Seattle Slew had a record value of $12 million.

If Seattle Slew had never raced at four, many of his critics would have continued to fault him for beating what they considered a bad bunch of three-year-olds in 1977. But in the late summer and fall of his four-year-old season he proved his greatness beyond a shadow of a doubt. Making his first start at four on May 14, Seattle Slew scored an 8¼-length victory in a seven-furlong Aqueduct allowance. Several days later, it was announced that he had suffered a hock injury in his stall. He didn't return to action until August 12, winning another seven-furlong allowance, this time by six lengths at Saratoga.

Following a second-place finish in the Paterson Handicap, Seattle Slew came back to win the Marlboro Cup by three lengths over Affirmed, the first meeting ever between two Triple Crown champions. "I've never been around a horse of this class," said Angel Cordero, Jr., who rode Seattle Slew in the Marlboro and for the rest of his career. "It's like flying an airplane."

Seattle Slew next won the 1¼-mile Woodward by four lengths over Exceller in two minutes flat without drawing a deep breath. Then, in an unforgettable performance, he ran second to Exceller in the Jockey Club Gold Cup at Belmont Park. "Never has a 'loser' gained more admirers in defeat," Russ Harris wrote in *The Thoroughbred Record*. "Many observers thought Seattle Slew would have done the impossible and won it all in a couple more jumps."

After six furlongs in 1:09⅖, a clocking that track

announcer Chic Anderson described to a national television audience as "unbelievable" in a 1½-mile race, Seattle Slew would have had every right to call it quits against Exceller, who had come with a rush from far off the pace and taken the lead in the homestretch. Seattle Slew, great horse that he was, dug in and battled back, but Exceller edged him by a nose. "I cried and cried and cried—not because he lost but because he tried so hard," said Karen Taylor.

This exciting racehorse made his final start in the 1⅛-mile Stuyvesant Handicap, triumphing by 3¼ lengths under 134 pounds, the heaviest weight of his career. "I only hope he does as well in his second life as he did in his first," a tearful Karen Taylor said in a thank-you over the Aqueduct public-address system. "It was a wonderful time, and we'll always remember it."

Seattle Slew, favored in every race except the Marlboro, won fourteen of his seventeen career starts. Cordero called Seattle Slew the best horse he ever rode. "He was the most talented one, the strongest one. He could run on any track with any weight at any distance." One reason for Seattle Slew's greatness was that he could have it both ways—he could run fast early and still have something left at the end. I don't know that I've ever seen another horse who could go that fast the first part of a race and keep on running.

Mickey Taylor believes that a mile was Seattle Slew's best distance. "I always thought he was a sprinter that forgot to stop," he said. "He could go a mile in thirty-three and change, but he just kept on going at the same speed."

Taylor said the Jockey Club Gold Cup probably was Seattle Slew's greatest race simply because he showed he could run that fast for six furlongs "and still be there at the end and then come back and one jump past the wire he was in front again." But he added, "Boy, I'll tell you, it's tough to throw out the Derby. He overcame a lot in the Derby to make it around there."

Did the Derby provide Taylor with his greatest thrill?

"No, probably the Champagne. I turned to Karen after the race and said, 'Man, this is a racehorse.' It's just hard to say. They're all such great races. And you can't throw out the Marlboro. Affirmed couldn't keep up, and he just distanced him."

Taylor made another interesting observation. "Everyone wants to make excuses, but the great ones overcome everyone," he said. "They overcome owners, trainers, jockeys, blacksmiths—you name it. When they're that good, they're good." Seattle Slew *was* that good.

Seattle Slew, who turned twenty-three in 1997, is standing at Three Chimneys Farm, Midway, Kentucky. He has sired many outstanding runners, including Swale, the 1984 Kentucky Derby winner. Another of Seattle Slew's sons, 1986 champion two-year-old colt Capote, sired Boston Harbor and Acceptable, the one-two finishers in the 1996 Breeders' Cup Juvenile.

The Taylors, who now reside in Ketchum, Idaho and Yakima, Washington, have the opportunity to see Seattle Slew about every three or four months. The old boy looks "fantastic" to Taylor. "He's getting a little bit lower in the back now, but his personality is still the same," he said. "To this day, I think he still does recognize Karen's voice." Seattle Slew is still going strong, having been bred to seventy-one mares in 1996, according to Taylor, the syndicate manager.

When a snowstorm hit central Kentucky in January 1996, Seattle Slew, who loves the snow, "came running up through that field, you know, twenty-two years old," Taylor recalled with a chuckle. "I'll tell you, he was moving, boy." Once a runner, always a runner—that's Seattle Slew, one of the best racehorses I've ever had the privilege of seeing.

W. SIMMS
Jockey

Willie Simms. (Photo courtesy Keeneland Library)

19

Willie Simms Perfect in the Derby

GEORGIA HAS PRODUCED many great athletes over the years, and one man ranking up there with the very best of them was none other than Willie Simms.

Willie who?

His name may not be a household word in Georgia these days, but back during his heyday in the latter part of the nineteenth century, Willie Simms was a great jockey. So talented was Simms that he won the only two runnings of the Kentucky Derby in which he ever rode, he starred in Europe as well as the United States, and in 1977 he was inducted into racing's Hall of Fame at Saratoga Springs, New York. He certainly left his mark on racing, standing out as one of the many gifted black riders of his era.

Simms earned his place in the Hall of Fame through a combination of natural ability and hard work. He had a certain instinct around horses and could communicate to them with his hands. A powerful finisher, he was a good bet in a close race. His own man, he rode with short stirrups that sometimes drew criticism. But he did things his way, and he did them extremely well.

This Georgia native traveled a long road to wind up in the Hall of Fame. It was a road that took him first to New York, where he was introduced to racing . . . to Kentucky, where he twice won the celebrated Derby . . . and to

Europe, where he made history and established himself as a truly international jockey.

Simms was born January 16, 1870 in Augusta, Georgia, and, as a youngster, was "greatly attracted by the gay colors of the jockeys' silks at the county fairs," wrote Marjorie R. Weber, the late racing historian from Louisville. "He determined then and there to become a rider. Without his parents' consent, he set out for New York."

Simms, "like the majority of Southern boys, manifested an early liking for horses, so that it may be said that turf life is really second nature to him," noted *The American Turf*, a book that came out in 1898. "After some preliminary association with horses he became attached to the stable of Mr. C. H. Pettingill, with whom he came East and remained some two years. The preliminary work that he went through was of such a character as to give him a sound knowledge of the primary details of his calling, and when the opportunity came to him to mount Saluda, the first horse that he ever rode, he was in perfect trim and admirably performed his duties."

Simms reportedly was picking up stray mounts in 1887 and 1888 in New York. It was in the latter year that he went to work for trainer Con Leighton, who conditioned horses for Cong. William L. Scott and admired Simms' ability for getting along with an especially obstinate horse. In 1889, Simms became what was termed "a full-fledged jockey on the big tracks." On May 15 of that year, he scored his first major victory, winning the half-mile Expectation Stakes by a length aboard Banquet, a 20-1 shot. Finishing second was the favored Belisarius, who was ridden by Eastern idol Edward ("Snapper") Garrison.

In the early 1890s, Simms rode on a free-lance basis before horseman Phil Dwyer engaged him for the 1892 season.

Simms ranked as the country's leading rider in total victories two straight years, winning 182 of 671 races in 1893 and

228 of 688 in 1894. Those indeed were very good years for Simms, who won the Belmont Stakes with Comanche in 1893 and then with Henry of Navarre in 1894. On August 31, 1893, he came through with a brilliant ride aboard Dobbins to finish in a dead heat with the great Domino in a famous match race. In 1894, besides his 228 triumphs (a career high), Simms boasted 163 second-place finishes and 128 thirds from his 688 mounts. His percentages of victories (33.1) and in-the-money finishes (75.4) that year were extremely high.

He was in such demand that in 1895 he had three employers, Mike Dwyer, Richard ("Boss") Croker, and P. J. Dwyer, who had first, second, and third call, respectively, on his services. His salary and fees for the year totaled more than twenty thousand dollars, "the greater part of which he saved and has safely invested," it was reported.

Simms went to England to ride for Mike Dwyer (Phil's brother) and Croker, showing the blokes on the other side of the Atlantic his ability and introducing a new riding style to that part of the racing world. He became the first native American jockey to triumph in a race in England on a horse whose owner, trainer, and entire outfit were Americans. While in England, he rode with a style that was foreign to that part of the world. With shortened stirrups, he rode far forward, crouched over the neck and the withers of his mounts. Simms was the first to show this style of riding to the British turf, and later another American, Todd Sloan, popularized it in England.

Simms' style was not exactly greeted with wild enthusiasm by the British. To be sure, he was laughed at.

In early 1895, *The Thoroughbred Record* magazine said of the jockey:

> The only fault that could ever be found with Simms as a jockey has been his partiality to ride with an extraordinary short stirrup, a style which gives him the appearance of a most unsightly seat. Simms, however, is

a perfect horseman, displaying the most excellent
judgment, especially on horses that require a lot of
coaxing and placing. He has beautiful hands and is
especially quick and clever in an emergency. Simms'
lowest weight last season was 105 pounds, but as a rule
he cannot ride under 107 pounds. It is purely a matter
of opinion, and may be a matter of sentiment, but
Simms, taken all around, is about the best jockey in
America to-day for, of the many seen in the saddle he
makes fewer mistakes and undoubtedly shows more
patience.

Simms' riding style was making news. Contrasting the
styles of U.S. and English riders, the *New York World* reported in 1895:

[The] conventional English seat [is] the customary
long rein and long stirrup. American jockeys use a
shorter stirrup and a tighter rein, although Simms exag-
gerates the prevailing type. In this country thoroughbreds are broken more roughly than in England and
their mouths are harder than the mounts of English
horses. The jockey there is not called upon to take so
tight a hold of his horse's head as are our jockeys.

Simms' style has often been discussed through the years,
but, interestingly enough, a photograph of him riding Ben
Brush to victory in the 1897 Suburban Handicap in New
York showed him with long stirrups and an upright position.
Even so, while riding in England, Simms' seat on a horse
made an impression, though unfavorable, with racing people there. However, Simms wasn't competing for blue rib-
bons in saddle-seat equitation—he was riding in horse
races, and, despite the criticism he received for the way he
looked in the saddle, he knew how to get the best results
from his mounts. *The American Turf* stated:

He remained in England four months, and while
there won some good races. He received great com-
mendation for his clever work, and his importance as a

jockey immediately rose in the estimation of turfmen, for it was more clearly shown than ever before that he was possessed of sound judgment, excellent foresight and undaunted courage. Many offers bidding for his services promptly came to him from both England and American owners, but he returned to America, and was welcomed as one of the turf heroes of the day.

Simms was at his best in the Kentucky Derby, twice winning the race in thrilling finishes—with Ben Brush in 1896 and with Plaudit two years later. In the '96 Derby, he rode Ben Brush to a narrow victory over Ben Eder. Ben Brush was a top-class horse, one who would be inducted into the Hall of Fame. Ben and Willie hit it off quite well together— great horse, great jockey, great combination.

The Thoroughbred Record (which misspelled the jockey's name, as did certain other publications in those days) reported: "It is true there were many spectators who honestly believe that Ben Eder won, but the obstruction offered by the judges' box makes it impossible for anybody but the judges or those in the timers' stand to tell, and there seems no doubt, from the statements of those in these positions, that Sims (as a great jockey will) saved just one more effort in Ben Brush, and using it in the last desperate leap, shot the hair on his nose in front of his shorter whiskered opponent."

M. Lewis Clark, one of the judges, said, "There was no doubt in the world about the finish. Simms simply lifted Brush a foot or so in front at the last jump."

In its account of that race, *The Courier-Journal* wrote:

> Willie Simms, covered with dust and smiles, and almost buried beneath a large bouquet of roses which had just been presented to him, was seen a few minutes after the race in the jockeys' dressing-room, and while he spoke modestly of his success it was easy to see that he was much elated over his victory. "Whew," he exclaimed, "that was a hot race, and don't you forget

it. I have ridden all kinds of races in this country and in England, but I had the finish of my life today.

"The only instructions I received was to win the race, and I did. I got off fairly well, but in the first 10 jumps Ben Brush stumbled and almost fell to his knees, nearly unseating me. But I gathered him up quickly and was in a good position as we passed the stand. First Mate was sailing out in front, but I did not fear him and closed up gradually, being second at the half-mile pole. Here I took a good hold on Ben and rounded the far turn running well in hand. First Mate was still in front, but I saw I had him beat, and for the first time I looked around. Perkins [James Perkins] on Semper Ego was close up, and Ben Eder was running like the devil.

"In a glance I saw that one of these two horses was the one I had to beat and let out a link and passed Thorpe [Charlie Thorpe, the jockey on First Mate]. My horse was running strong and true as we rounded the bend for home, but I hardly had gone 50 yards before he began to tire and at the eighth pole, where he was joined by Ben Eder, he was in trouble and I went to the bat. From that time on I rode him with whip and spur—and, my, how he did stand it. He ran true, stood his punishment well and we won. He is the gamest horse I ever threw a leg over."

Asked how far he won the race, Simms replied, "About that far," measuring to the elbow on his left arm.

The Courier-Journal reported that Snapper Garrison, the famous white jockey of that era, "has said that Sims [*sic*] was the best finisher now riding on the American turf, and those who saw him lift Ben Brush from the one-sixteenth pole to the wire and land him a winner will doubtless fully agree with the 'Snapper.'"

Two years later in the Derby, Simms piloted Plaudit to a nose victory over Lieber Karl. Plaudit, owned by the noted turfman John E. Madden, carried 117 pounds, compared with 122 on Lieber Karl. The difference in weights no doubt had a bearing on the outcome of the race, but so did Simms' flawless ride.

Following that race, *The Courier-Journal* reported:

> Jockey Simms was of course elated over his second brilliant victory in the Kentucky Derby. Two years ago he landed Ben Brush a winner in one of the closest finishes in the history of the Kentucky classic, and although he has crossed the ocean and made his name famous in England as well as in the most noted of America's fixed events, he seemed yesterday to be just as well pleased over winning the Kentucky Derby of 1898 as a green stable boy would have been. It was a victory that he can well afford to be proud of, for if a horse was ever handled in a masterful manner it was Plaudit in yesterday's race. But while Simms was elated over his victory he was not at all boastful about it, and did not underrate the abilities of the riders who were contending against him.

In its account of the 1898 Derby, *The Louisville Commercial* reported:

> [Simms] was followed to the paddock by an excited, cheering crowd after he had weighed out. Sims [*sic*] has won many a great race, and was not greatly elated over his victory, though he was naturally proud of adding another such laurel to his list. In the dressing room he was overwhelmed with congratulations, which he took easily. Sims is a very modest young fellow and had little to say. To a Commercial reporter Sims said: "I was confident of winning all along, because I thought I had the best horse. I was told to ride him for all he was worth, and I did it. Lieber Karl pushed me hard, and once in the back stretch it looked to me as though he would win the race. It was a terrible fight all the way around. The extra five pounds, I think, beat Karl."

He was quoted in *The Courier-Journal* as saying:

> Plaudit wobbled a bit just after we had straightened away for the run home, and I had to steady him down a little before I could call on him again, but when I did he went forward. By this time we were coming to the last eighth, and even then I did not know whether I had a chance to win or not, but after we passed the eighth pole I saw that Lieber Karl was beginning to quit and I knew I had the race won. I want to say right now, and I believe the other boys in the race will back me up, that a horse never ran a gamer race than Plaudit ran today.

The following month Simms won the Preakness, triumphing aboard Sly Fox by two lengths.

The Thoroughbred Record, in its September 1, 1900 issue, reported:

> Willie Sims [*sic*], who in the opinion of that peerless horseman, the late Byron McClelland, was classified as the best jockey in America in 1895 and 1896, will accompany Tod Sloan [*sic*] on his return to England. Sims has come into little luck since Mr. Philip Dwyer fell out with him in 1897, and that difference with Mr. Dwyer has seemingly undone the great jockey. On the other side, where he is no stranger, having been there with Mr. M. F. Dwyer's horses only a few years ago, Sims will likely do well, for while the American mode of riding at that time he was in England, was the object of ridicule of English horsemen, the whole aspect of affairs has been changed by the successes of Sloan, the two Reiffs, Martin and Rigby, until now good riders from this side are in popular demand.

Records aren't complete for Simms' entire career, but it is believed that he won with approximately 25 percent of his mounts, a high figure.

With all too many jockeys throughout history (particularly in the early days), it was a case of easy come, easy go and they squandered the money that they earned, but not so with Simms, who saved his money and made sound real-estate investments. He was said to be one of the wealthiest jockeys on the turf. In the early part of this century, the financially comfortable Simms retired as a rider and began training horses, a job that he continued as late as 1924.

At the age of fifty-seven, Simms died of pneumonia on February 26, 1927, in Asbury Park, New Jersey. A bachelor, he lived with his widowed mother. Fifty years after his death, Simms was inducted into the Hall of Fame. "One of the greatest jockeys America produced in the 19th century, his accomplishments have too long remained in the shadows of time," *Daily Racing Form* executive columnist Joe Hirsch wrote before the induction of Willie Simms (1870-1927), riding legend.

20

Unbridled Blossomed at the Derby

FRANCES A. GENTER HAD BEEN INVOLVED in the Thoroughbred business for a half-century, but not until 1990 did she ever have a starter in the Kentucky Derby. For a variety of reasons, such Genter stars as Rough'n Tumble, In Reality, Superbity, and Dr. Carter didn't make it to Churchill Downs on the first Saturday in May. But the ninety-two-year-old Mrs. Genter finally had her silks go to the post in the 116th Derby, and Unbridled brought her light blue and yellow colors home on top in a decisive 3½-length victory before 128,257 fans who turned out in cool weather.

Summer Squall was the runner-up, marking the third straight year that jockey Pat Day has finished second in America's premier horse race. The favored Mister Frisky, who entered the Derby unbeaten in sixteen starts, came in eighth in the field of fifteen.

Derby Day is a major attraction in Louisville, turning the city upside down and inside out for an event hailed as "the greatest two minutes in sports." Tulips and wallets have a way of unfolding at the same time at Churchill Downs as thousands of racing people from all over the world converge on Louisville for this great race.

Like the tulips that blossom at Derby time, Unbridled was blooming in the days leading up to the race. If there was ever a "now" horse for the Derby, it was Unbridled in 1990. On the eve of the race, with a hard rain coming down at

Churchill Downs, trainer Carl Nafzger stood inside his barn and talked about how well Unbridled was doing. "He's doing good," said Nafzger, a former rodeo bull rider. "He's happy. He's not worried about anything. He's training good. He's coming into the race good."

Unbridled had three good workouts at Churchill Downs—a half-mile in :51⅕ on April 22, six furlongs in 1:13 on April 25, and five furlongs in 1:01⅘ on May 1. "He trained superb over these grounds ever since the Blue Grass," his jockey, Craig Perret, said after the Derby. "He's made every step and every bridge we put to him to get here. He let us know the whole time he was getting better. He did it professionally, and that's why he won the way he did today."

Unbridled had worked so satisfactorily that Nafzger said on Derby Eve, "He's taken all of my excuses away. Now if it rains, the Good Lord might give me another one."

Rain (only a trace) did come on Derby Day, but it stopped in time for the Derby and, to the delight of the crowd, the sun was out for the big race. The track had been rated muddy for the first six races on the card but was upgraded to good for the Derby.

Unbridled then went out there and came home in 2:02 for the mile and one-quarter, bettering Venetian Way's 2:02⅖ on a good track in 1960 for the fastest time on an off track in the history of the Derby. With Perret hitting him eight times right-handed coming down the stretch, Unbridled covered the last quarter of a mile in slightly faster than 24⅖ seconds, an excellent finish.

This was the same Unbridled who was criticized for winning the Florida Derby in a slow 1:52. But astute racing people noted that Unbridled had gone from third at the stretch call to a convincing four-length victory in the Florida Derby. Many of these same people knew, too, that Unbridled was blossoming at the Downs, that he was right on top of running the race of his life.

Listed at 12-1 in the program's morning line, Unbridled went off at 10-1. Mister Frisky was the 1.90-1 favorite, with Summer Squall the 2.10-1 second choice. Thirty Six Red, the Wood Memorial winner, had solid backing at 5-1, and Arkansas Derby winner Silver Ending was 6-1. Trainer D. Wayne Lukas had a three-horse entry (Land Rush, Real Cash, and Power Lunch) that was 14-1. The other starters were higher than 30-1.

Mrs. Genter attended the Derby, and sitting in a box with Nafzger, she was informed by her trainer of Unbridled's progress during the running of the race. As many had predicted, with so much legitimate speed in the race, this Derby would be set up for a horse coming from off the pace, and Mrs. Genter had to like what she heard from Nafzger as Unbridled, eleventh the first time past the wire, improved his position going down the backstretch.

Nearing the quarter pole, Summer Squall had moved into the lead, but the long-striding Unbridled was coming on. "I was not sure if I had Pat's horse at the five-sixteenths pole yet," Perret said. "I did not know if I would beat him at that point, but I knew I was going to be the one to put all the pressure on him. It was going to come down to be me and Pat. When I got to the quarter pole, I had looped up on him pretty easy and I saw Pat when he went to hit his horse left-handed. He was still right there next to me, and I said, 'You're in trouble.' I think I got a little more energy at that point, too. I said, 'Boy, this is great!'"

Down the stretch charged the blaze-faced Unbridled, who overtook Summer Squall in a move that had Nafzger excitedly telling Mrs. Genter, "He's taking the lead! He's gonna win! He's gonna win! He's gonna win! He's a winner! He's a winner, Mrs. Genter! You've won the Kentucky Derby, Mrs. Genter. I love you."

Indeed, Unbridled was a winner—and a most deserving one. Much the best, he produced a victory that was quite popular with racing people. Mrs. Genter has been racing horses for so many years that it seemed only fitting that she should finally win this classic. Taken to the winner's circle in a wheelchair, she was delighted with her colt's brilliant effort. Nafzger later said, "I just made a comment a couple three times this week on radio and television and newspapers, if I ever won a Kentucky Derby, I wish it'd be this Kentucky Derby because I would like to win it for Mrs. Genter."

Mrs. Genter purchased Unbridled as a weanling from breeder Tartan Farms' dispersal for $70,000. Sired by Fappiano and out of the La Fabuleux mare Gana Facil, Unbridled became the fifth Florida-bred to win the Derby, joining Needles (1956), Carry Back (1961), Foolish Pleasure (1975), and Affirmed (1978).

Summer Squall, who bled earlier in 1990, made it to the Derby under the expert handling of trainer Neil Howard and "had a flawless trip," said Day. The jockey did say that the Dogwood Stable colt, turning for home in the lead, lost his concentration when he was distracted by the huge crowd on both sides of the track. "I think my colt could have made it a bit more of a horse race if he had just maintained his attention span at the head of the stretch," Day said. "He just kinda lost concentration momentarily and never seemed to regain that. When you turn into that stretch, it's something you don't experience any other time. Coming off the turn, he was by himself, he was quite relaxed at that point, and all of a sudden the roar, and he momentarily lost it. I think it shook him up just a little bit. He just lost his composure, and that's so unlike him. He's always been *so* composed."

Day knew how Eddie Arcaro felt in 1942 when he chose Devil Diver over Shut Out in the Derby. (Shut Out won.) He also understands how Bill Shoemaker felt in 1964 when he chose Hill Rise over Northern Dancer for the Derby. (Northern Dancer won.) And he knows how Braulio Baeza felt in 1967 when he chose to ride Successor instead of Proud Clarion in the Derby. (Proud Clarion won.)

With his choice of the two mounts, Day chose Summer Squall over Unbridled for the Derby.

"I'm not one to second guess myself," Day said afterward in the jockeys' room. "I was confident and comfortable coming into this race on the colt that I had decided to ride. I have absolutely no misgivings about that whatsoever."

Watching Nafzger on the television rerun "keeping Mrs. Genter abreast of where their colt was at brought tears to my eyes," Day added. "She's been in the business a long time, and I congratulate her. I couldn't understand why I lost until I seen Mrs. Genter win. Maybe it just wasn't meant for us to win today. It was obviously meant for her to win."

Summer Squall finished a full six lengths in front of Pleasant Tap, a 40-1 long shot. The first three finishers all prepped at Keeneland Race Course that spring—Summer Squall and Unbridled running first and third, respectively, in the Blue Grass and Pleasant Tap finishing second in the Lexington Stakes.

"The goal wasn't to have him 100 percent to win the Blue Grass," Perret said of Unbridled. "The goal was to win the Kentucky Derby."

Pleasant Tap, who gave an excellent account of himself for a colt who had missed considerable training earlier in the spring, was three lengths in front of Video Ranger, a 65-1 shot. Silver Ending finished fifth, marking the fourth straight Triple Crown race in which trainer Ron McAnally had been fifth. In 1989, Hawkster ran fifth in the Derby, Preakness, and Belmont for McAnally.

Later in the year, Unbridled captured the Breeders' Cup Classic at Belmont Park by a length. He was voted champion three-year-old colt.

When Unbridled retired in the fall of 1991, he had a record of eight victories, six seconds, and six thirds from twenty-four starts and earnings of $4,489,475, fifth highest on the all-time list and tops for a Florida-bred. "It has been quite a three years," Nafzger said at the time of Unbridled's retirement. "I've enjoyed every bit of it. It was a great honor and thrill. It's unbelievable what this one horse has done. I'm gonna miss him a bunch. You don't have a good friend for a long time and then he goes home and you don't miss him. Unbridled is what you'd always want. You'd always want the perfect horse. He never did bite anybody, he never did kick anybody, he had a great attitude, he loved people, loved kids—and when you asked him to run, he ran. He'd always give us his race. We'll miss him a lot, but at the same time we're happy that he went to stud. Now he's got an opportunity to be a top stallion. He deserves it."

Unbridled is proving to be a top stallion. He sired 1996 Kentucky Derby winner Grindstone.

21

Strike the Gold
Was Bred to Do It

IT WAS IN 1991 that Strike the Gold came through with a strong finishing kick to win the Kentucky Derby and to give the Dosage Index system a swift kick in the pants.

The three-year-old colt became the second son of Alydar to capture the Run for the Roses, and he did it in splendid fashion, rushing up on the outside in the stretch to triumph before a lighthearted crowd of 135,554 that included Gen. H. Norman Schwarzkopf.

More than a few otherwise knowledgeable bettors discounted Strike the Gold's chances in the $905,800 Derby, simply because he didn't have the Dosage Index number, a silly formula that somehow professes to predict whether a horse's pedigree is slanted toward speed or stamina. Since 1929, every Derby winner has had a Dosage Index of not over 4.00 . . . until Strike the Gold came along. His Dosage Index was 9.00.

So much for Dosage.

Strike the Gold, out of the Hatchet Man mare Majestic Gold, rallied from twelfth in the crowded field to win in 2:03 on a fast track. Alysheba, also sired by Alydar, won the 1987 Derby in 2:03²/₅.

With trainer Nick Zito bringing him up to the race in top shape and jockey Chris Antley making the right moves in the race, Strike the Gold was in the best of hands for this 117th Derby. Moreover, this colt had the breeding, in spite of what his Dosage had to say about the matter.

Commenting on Dosage during Derby Week, Zito said, "I call it witchcraft. Somebody will beat it someday. This horse looks exactly like his daddy. He's his daddy's son. If genetics mean anything, they mean like father like son. His daddy ran *extremely well* in all the Triple Crown races. And let's not take anything away from his poor mother. His mother won the Pocahontas [a division in 1981] right here at Churchill Downs."

Alydar wasn't able to win any of the Triple Crown races in 1978, but he ran his heart out in finishing second to Affirmed each time. In retirement, Alydar proved to be a tremendous success at stud, siring such stars as Alysheba, Criminal Type, Easy Goer, Althea, Turkoman, and Strike the Gold.

Strike the Gold was sold by Calumet Farm in September 1990 for an undisclosed sum in a seven-horse package deal to the three-man partnership of B. Giles Brophy, William J. Condren, and Joseph M. Cornacchia. Strike the Gold, who was unraced at the time, was the only two-year-old in the package, the others being yearlings. On November 15, 1990, Alydar was put down at Calumet Farm, and later that day Strike the Gold, in his third start, broke his maiden at Aqueduct.

As one writer put it, "In a sense, Alydar had left the same day one of his colts had arrived."

Indeed, Strike the Gold had arrived, but he was still a young horse, still learning what this business of racing was all about. Under the supervision of Zito, he began to develop.

Still, he had his detractors, some of whom pointed out before the Derby that he had won just two of seven career starts. What they failed to observe was that he was improving with each race and that he had won the Blue Grass Stakes by a resounding three lengths over Fly So Free, the Derby favorite at the time. Moreover, Strike the Gold ran the last three-eighths in the Blue Grass in an impressive 35.5 seconds.

The morning line for the Derby established Fly So Free as the 5-2 favorite, but the bettors at Churchill Downs didn't see it that way. They wagered heavily on Hansel, who was coming into the race off impressive triumphs in the Jim Beam Stakes at Turfway Park and the Lexington Stakes at Keeneland. In both of those races, however, Hansel faced rather weak opposition, and it came as a surprise to many that he would be favored at 5-2 in this 117th Derby.

Fly So Free was the 3.30-1 second choice, followed by Strike the Gold at 4.80-1 and Best Pal at 5.20-1.

These four horses made up the Derby's Big Four, and many so-called experts didn't see any other legitimate contenders in the race. As it turned out, Mane Minister, an 86-1 long shot, gave an excellent account of himself in finishing third, and Green Alligator, relegated to running in the mutuel field, made up plenty of ground in the homestretch in finishing a flying fourth—which just goes to show how much the experts know. And when it came to Strike the Gold, those who had been carefully watching his progress since he arrived in Kentucky on March 30 knew that he was coming up to the race in perfect fashion.

Zito, whose main stable was based in New York, stayed with Strike the Gold in Kentucky every step of the way. Zito was a man on a mission, and he had the horse with the ability, the heart, and, of course, the stamina. It seemed to this writer that all Zito needed was for Strike the Gold to avoid traffic problems in the Derby, and the roses were his.

A fun-loving crowd turned out in pleasant, though somewhat humid, weather for the 1991 Derby. The gathering included the usual array of celebrities, but this renewal had a special attraction in General Schwarzkopf, commander of Operation Desert Storm. Occasionally, he would wave to the crowd, and the fans loved it, waving back, shouting, and taking pictures of this American hero. People who otherwise aren't turned on by celebrities tried desperately to get a glimpse of the general. He was the man of the hour at the

Derby . . . and Strike the Gold was the horse of the hour. Afterward, General Schwarzkopf said, "They told me they were going to win before the race, so I knew what was going to happen. But it was a great campaign and a great winner."

As the Derby unfolded, Sea Cadet, as expected, went to the lead. Running second in the early going was Forty Something, who was ridden by Andrea Seefeldt, the third female jockey in Derby history. Strike the Gold was far back as the field thundered past the finish line for the first time. The opening quarter was run in 23⅕ seconds, and as the field straightened away for the charge down the backstretch, the first half-mile was timed in :46⅖.

With six furlongs in 1:11⅕, Strike the Gold had moved up to tenth at the half-mile pole. "Coming to the turn, horses started to bunch up a little bit," Antley said. "Strike the Gold's not the kind of horse that drags you up there. You kinda have to urge him to do it. He responded well."

Caught in close quarters between horses near the end of the backstretch, Strike the Gold was guided to the outside, where he wouldn't encounter any traffic jams. Rounding the far turn and approaching the quarter pole, it seemed to be anybody's Derby. Sea Cadet was still in front with a quarter of a mile to go, but Fly So Free, Corporate Report, Mane Minister, and Hansel were racing side by side in close pursuit.

Strike the Gold was charging up on the outside, and Antley sensed that the roses were his. "I think I was already grinning at the time coming to the quarter pole," he said.

While Antley was grinning, the crowd was cheering wildly as the field came down the stretch. Best Pal, who had broken from the number-fifteen post position, found room along the rail and came surging through in a gallant effort. But he couldn't overtake Strike the Gold, who had taken command on the outside.

"He has this habit of not switching leads," Antley said, "and that was the main thing he did last time that made him beat Fly So Free. And as soon as we went on and I went by the horses, the first time I hit him he went right over to his right lead and finished up strong."

Near the end, Strike the Gold drifted out under left-handed whipping. "I was hoping that he'd drift a little faster than he'd run forward," said Gary Stevens, the jockey on Best Pal. "But it didn't happen that way."

Trainer Ian Jory said that Best Pal "didn't get the perfect trip," but Stevens described it as a "dream trip."

Said Stevens, who didn't use Best Pal's number-fifteen post position as an excuse, "They were lined up six wide going into the final turn, and I just held my position, stayed where I was. I had a ton of horse underneath me. I didn't want to move until the quarter pole. I wanted a strong last quarter in him, and it opened up beautifully at the quarter pole. When I got through inside the eighth pole, I thought I was a winner. There were about five horses in the race at that time, and I knew it was going to be tight."

Stevens saw "a flash on the outside." He didn't know that it was Strike the Gold, but he knew the horse was flying. "I kept thinking all the way that final sixteenth that I had a shot of catching him—the way he was drifting out," Stevens said. "My horse had his mind on running and was giving me everything he had and we were steadily getting there. But there wasn't enough time, and I don't know if we would have got him if we had gone around again. Really no excuses. Just very proud of the way he ran."

Asked whether Best Pal saw Strike the Gold on the outside, Stevens replied, "I truly don't believe that my horse *did* see him out there, but I can also say in the same breath that my horse was giving his all. My horse is not a cheating type. He's not the type of horse to wait on another horse. I definitely don't want to place the blame on him not being able to see the other horse out in the middle of the track, because he was digging down and trying, giving me everything that he had."

Besides Strike the Gold, Alydar also sired two other winners on the 1991 Derby Day card—Foresta, who triumphed
in the race before the Derby, the Capitol Holding Mile, for
the second straight year, and Greydar (a full brother to
Strike the Gold), who captured the race after the Derby.

Strike the Gold was bred by Calumet Farm, which had
bred eight previous Derby winners. As Zito put it, Strike
the Gold was "raised in a palace" at Calumet, the world-
famous farm in the heart of the Bluegrass. He was raised in
a palace, and he was certainly bred to win at a mile and a
quarter.

22

Go for Gin "Knew the Way"

As STRIKE THE GOLD CAME ROLLING down the stretch to win the 1991 Kentucky Derby, the colt's trainer, Nick Zito, kept yelling, "Show me the way!" On May 7, 1994, as Go for Gin charged down the stretch to win the Kentucky Derby, Zito screamed repeatedly, "We know the way!" Go for Gin, ridden expertly by Chris McCarron, certainly knew the way home in the 120th Derby, arriving there ahead of thirteen opponents before a crowd of 130,594 at historic Churchill Downs. Zito himself knew the way to the Derby winner's circle, having appeared there twice in four years.

In Go for Gin, Zito had a colt who was primed for his best effort. As Zito said before the Derby, "He's going to run the race of his life." Go for Gin did just that, winning the Derby by two lengths over the late-running Strodes Creek on a sloppy track.

Intermittent heavy rains fell on Derby Day, subsiding about an hour before the big race, and the sloppy track was to Go for Gin's liking. He had raced on off tracks five previous times in his career, with two victories and three seconds to his credit. But even if the track had been dry for the Derby, Go for Gin was going to run a strong race. He simply was that good on that particular day.

As the horses were led over from the stable area to the paddock for the Derby, the big Strodes Creek was on his toes and looking sharp. The favored Holy Bull, on the other hand, had his head down as he neared the paddock tunnel and didn't look like the same horse who had won the Blue Grass Stakes by 3½ lengths three weeks earlier. He didn't run like that horse either.

Nobody could know that Holy Bull wasn't going to run his race in the Derby, and speculation among certain people was that this long-striding gray colt would take an early lead and have things his own way. "We want to stay a little off Holy Bull," Zito said beforehand. "Just follow him. I'd like for McCarron to stay a length or two off." Zito also said that he wanted Go for Gin "to take the first crack at Holy Bull on the backstretch."

As it turned out, Holy Bull was a no-show on the front end, and Go for Gin led for much of this eventful race. Holy Bull, a winner in seven of eight previous races and sent off at 2.20-1 in the Derby, didn't get off to a good start. "My horse stands in the gate fine," the colt's owner-trainer, W. A. ("Jimmy") Croll, said after the Derby. "He stands there like a soldier."

But, for whatever reason, Holy Bull wasn't standing at attention in the gate. Instead, he was swinging his head around and wasn't anxious to break. After a tardy start, he was pinched between Ulises and Powis Castle.

Brocco, the second choice at 4.30-1, also failed to get off well. "He was looking up in the grandstand, stargazing," said his jockey, Gary Stevens. "He just walked from the gate." But the Derby is a long race—a full mile and one-quarter—and if a horse is good enough, he should overcome a slow start.

The horse with a real excuse was Valiant Nature, who almost went down in a race so roughly run that it was called the Demolition Derby.

The overmatched Ulises, who had absolutely no business running in the Derby and caused all kinds of problems while being loaded into the starting gate, held a short lead the first time by the wire. Go for Gin, who ducked out into

Tabasco Cat after the start, was running second, just a head behind Ulises after the opening quarter-mile. Holy Bull was a colt with tremendous natural speed, but he was back in sixth place after the first quarter. Brocco was ninth. Smilin Singing Sam also got away slowly and didn't show his usual early speed.

On the first turn, an incident took place that ruined any chance that Valiant Nature might have had. Valiant Nature, with no place to go, jumped the heels of Holy Bull, and his rider, Laffit Pincay, Jr., struggled to stay aboard. Pincay, rightly or wrongly, blamed Powis Castle for coming out and causing the problem. "He was running straight and then all of a sudden just came out," Pincay said.

Pincay had to take up sharply, and Valiant Nature sliced to the outside into the path of Strodes Creek. The incident caused Strodes Creek to swerve to the outside and, in the process, impede Meadow Flight, who wound up in the middle of the racetrack. That problem forced Strodes Creek to alter course somewhat, but he didn't lose nearly as much ground as some observers suggested.

Following a snappy opening quarter-mile in 22⅘ seconds, Go for Gin moved to the lead and took the field through comfortable fractions of :47⅕ for the half-mile, 1:11⅘ for the six furlongs, and 1:37⅗ for the mile.

Near the three-sixteenths pole, another scary incident took place, this one far back in the pack. Southern Rhythm drifted out toward Meadow Flight, who proceeded to come out into Mahogany Hall's path. Mahogany Hall, who apparently clipped heels, nearly went down while being turned sideways. He somehow recovered from that incident and came in ninth. This game colt, who no doubt would have finished closer had it not been for that mishap, came out of the Derby with a wrenched left hind ankle.

As for Go for Gin, he had clear sailing and led by a length or a length and a half at the quarter pole and by 4 or 4½ lengths at the eighth pole. Strodes Creek, seventh after

a mile, made a rally in the homestretch, but this plodding
sort of a runner wasn't going to catch Go for Gin, who
coasted home on top and had plenty left at the wire.
Blumin Affair, who always seemed to be coming on in his
races, rallied and finished third, followed by Brocco, who
had moved up to second or third at the stretch call before
fading to fourth at the wire. Soul of the Matter, who didn't
have a clear path all the way, finished fifth, followed in
order by Tabasco Cat, Southern Rhythm, Powis Castle,
Mahogany Hall, Smilin Singing Sam, Meadow Flight, Holy
Bull, Valiant Nature, and the useless Ulises, who trailed Go
for Gin by all of 35¼ lengths.

Go for Gin, owned by William Condren and Joseph
Cornacchia, was timed in 2:03⅗ for the mile and one-quarter. Listed at odds of 15-1 in the morning line, the colt went
off at 9.10-1.

Although only a handful of writers picked Go for Gin to
win the Derby, he figured to run a good race. McCarron,
who had never been aboard Go for Gin until a workout six
days before the Derby, fit the free-running colt like a glove
and let him do his thing on the first Saturday in May. That
is, he let him have his head and run.

Where Holy Bull's pedigree left many observers question-
ing whether he could go a mile and a quarter, Go for Gin
clearly had the breeding to handle the Derby distance. By
Cormorant out of Never Knock, the colt is a half-brother to
Pleasant Tap. Go for Gin already had run in three 1⅛-mile
races before the Derby—an 8½-length victory in the 1993
Remsen, a fourth in the Florida Derby on March 12, 1994,
and a second in the Wood Memorial on April 16, 1994.

Unlike certain lightly raced Derby starters, Go for Gin
had a solid foundation, having started nine times. He con-
sistently ran good races, boasting four victories and three
seconds before the Derby.

Besides everything that was obvious on paper in Go for
Gin's past performances, there was the all-important fact

that he was coming up to the Derby in splendid fashion. "This horse took to that track," Zito said the morning after the Derby. "He gave us two and a half weeks of unbelievable training."

This 120th Derby was perceived by some as a wide-open race with as many as eight starters having a chance to win, but that appraisal was far from accurate. No Derby has ever had that many candidates good enough to win. Usually, just a few horses surface to the top by Derby Day with a solid chance in the Run for the Roses. Go for Gin was one of those, and this colt with speed and stamina proved it on Derby Day.

Dan Mangeot, president and chief executive officer of the Kentucky Derby Festival until his death in 1997. (Photo courtesy the Kentucky Derby Festival)

23

The Kentucky Derby Festival Has Come a Long Way, Baby

IF THE KENTUCKY DERBY FESTIVAL ever establishes a museum, attention should first focus on a column written by Earl Ruby in *The Courier-Journal*. In his "Ruby's Report" column appearing on Sunday, February 19, 1956, this legendary sports editor informed his readers of the following:

> Another effort is being made to provide a full week of fun for Kentucky Derby visitors. . . . The first try, about 25 years ago, was born a quarter of a century too soon, say fathers of the new plan.
>
> Louisville is not the same tired old town it used to be. Sick and tired of being sick and tired, it has spruced up and is yelling for nourishment. This time the festival will succeed, they promise.
>
> The first move will be made this spring. It will be a giant parade of floats, marching bands and prancing horses. A sort of history of the horse race, put to music and flowers. And the story of industry and commerce told by the ingenuity of the floatmakers.
>
> Addison McGhee, public relations man with wide experience in such undertakings, is considering an invitation to serve as general chairman of the parade. . . . Mayor Andy Broaddus has agreed to serve an honorary chairman. Jim Stewart is vice chairman. . . . K.P. Vinsel, executive director of the Louisville Chamber of Commerce, Stanley Hugenberg, executive vice-

president of Churchill Downs, and Ray Wimberg, a
member of the C. of C. sports committee, are among
those on the working committee.

The theme of the parade, they believe, should be
the industrial history of the city as told by successive
floats coupled with renewals of the thoroughbred race.

Mayor's Ideas—Mayor Broaddus said yesterday he
thinks Derby Week would not be complete without big
name dance bands at the two leading hotels, a TV boxing card in the new Fairgrounds Coliseum, and some
outstanding night baseball attraction.

The parade, he thinks, probably should be staged
on Thursday evening, rather than Friday, because of
the pressure of other events on Friday.

It has been suggested that the parade wind up at
Churchill Downs, circling the track once before dis-
banding. And that seats in the club house be sold
through the Junior League or similar organizations,
for charitable work.

Thus was born the Kentucky Derby Festival.

Ruby was one of the four founders, along with Wimberg,
McGhee (public-relations director for Brown-Forman), and
Basil Caummisar (promotions and public-relations director
for *The Courier-Journal* and *The Louisville Times*). Let us go
back in festival history and relive some of the moments of
this grand event.

Wimberg's Dream: A Parade for the Poor

Ruby, who served as sports editor of *The Courier-Journal*
for thirty years (1938-68), recalled that the late Wimberg
"deserves a lot of credit for the start of the parade." Ruby
related: "Ray said, 'The parade I want is a parade for the
poor people who can't get in to see the Derby.'" Wimberg's
idea was that the parade would be made up of homemade
floats.

"High-school bands or maybe junior-high-school bands,"

Ruby said. "Have the schools build their own floats—just everything homemade. My first argument was it was going to cost money.

"'Well, this won't cost money,' Ray said. 'If we do it right, it won't cost any money.' I said, 'Well, I don't know, Ray.'

"If I had said no to that then, there probably would never have been a Derby Festival as we know it today. But as we sat there and discussed it, I said, 'Well, let's take a try. Let's take a chance on it—see what we can do.'"

The Ultimate Salute to the Festival

In a 1995 interview, Ruby said, "I often shudder at the thought of what would have happened to the festival as we know it today if, when Ray came to me in my office and we talked this over, I had said to him, as so many in the past had said, 'No, Ray, it's a bum idea. I don't think we should try it.' But that didn't happen."

Ruby covered many major athletic events and was instrumental in promoting sports. But when it comes to his many achievements, he won't talk about sports or games. No, he won't mention hoops or horses. Instead, he'll single out his role in the founding of the Derby Festival as his greatest achievement.

He modestly said that his "little part in the start of the festival and the push I gave it" exceeds everything else combined that he accomplished in his thirty years as sports editor. All that doesn't give him "the pleasure and the pride that I get in what I did to start this *terrific* thing that now is so prominent in Louisville," he said. "For thirty years combined, you can add them all up and they won't add up to just that one column on the festival and my pushing on through when nobody else would at times." For those who know what Earl Ruby accomplished during his distinguished career, those remarks are the single greatest tribute that could ever be paid the festival.

Great Steamboat Race News
across the Pond

Recalling his early work with the festival, Caummisar said, "The Great Steamboat Race, in my opinion, had interest only to people along the river that knew what a steamboat would be. All of us were volunteers and we'd work during the day for our daily bread and then at night we'd do whatever we had to do for the Derby Festival. I'd sit there and type out the addresses of the sports editors up and down the Ohio and Mississippi rivers and send out releases about the upcoming Great Steamboat Race.

"I thought maybe we'd enlist something from St. Louis and New Orleans or somewhere but nothing like the surprise I got when somebody sent me a four-column picture of the Great Steamboat Race on page 1 of the *New York Herald-Tribune* Paris edition. Now that was more space than 90 percent of the papers in the United States gave us. But the people from Paris were enamored of the idea of two paddle-wheel steamboats going down the Ohio River. And that's when we really began to realize the value of the thing."

Martha Layne: A Festival Queen

The Derby Festival Queen in 1959 was Martha Layne Hall, and a caption underneath a photograph of her riding on a parade float said, "The large tissue-paper crown above her throne kept some of the rain off Her Highness, who two days before was ill with food-poisoning during a visit to Washington."

This Derby Queen would later stand on the presentation stand at the Derby as the governor of Kentucky . . . Martha Layne Collins herself.

Who's That Sandy-haired Guy, Anyway?

In one of those now-it-can-be-told stories, Jack Guthrie (festival executive vice-president from 1971 to 1977) revealed: "A funny thing, Glen Campbell was supposed to be the grand marshal when he was coming in for the Philip Morris show one year. It was bad weather—raining and whatever—and the plane was circling. The parade was going down the street, and his plane was still circling."

Wheeler Rudd, a festival director, had "sandy red hair—not unlike, from a distance, Glen Campbell's," Guthrie went on to explain. "So this Cadillac—and it was closed—went by and here's Wheeler waving out of this doggone Cadillac with Glen Campbell's name on its side. I'm sitting on a review stand wondering what in the world's going on. Wheeler figured, What else am I going to do? I gotta do something. Well, I'll just get in here and ride down and wave.

"I don't recall that this was publicized. No, we got away with that one, I guess."

Keep Those Coupons Coming

Dan Mangeot, the festival's president and chief executive officer until his death in 1997, liked to tell a story about coupons. "We had Spalding golf balls come to the festival in 1985," he said. "They wanted to introduce a new golf ball in the market. We said, 'We've got the perfect vehicle for you. Put a coupon in our Pegasus Pin program, and they can redeem it for a free golf ball.' Their salesman said, 'No, we're gonna give away a sleeve of golf balls.' I said, 'Fine. What's your average return on a coupon program that you do?' He said, 'Oh, 7 to 10 percent.' I said, 'Guess what? Ours is up in the 40s.' The guy said, 'No way.' I said, 'Okay. How much do you have budgeted for this project?' He said, 'We got it covered. We want to be in.'

"So they're in [the coupon program]. Halfway through the festival, I get a call in the office. It's not the salesman I dealt with. It's the president of Spalding Sporting Goods, and he said, 'What's going on down there?' I said, 'Pardon me?' He said, 'I'm giving away 75,000 golf balls, I got twelve people working overtime, and I got more coupons than I know what to do with.' I said, 'Hey, we told you.' They budgeted the project at $25,000 and wound up spending over $125,000 redeeming the coupons."

All about the General

One of the most distinguished celebrities ever to attend the Derby was H. Norman Schwarzkopf, who was parade marshal in 1991. Mangeot normally didn't go down the parade route. But with Schwarzkopf on hand, he made an exception.

"I had to go down the parade route with the general because we were taking him from there to the Philip Morris Concert of Stars," Mangeot said. "I was in a police car in front of him, and we were riding down the street and I heard this enormous roar. I said, 'What is that?' And it dawned on me. I looked around, and there was a Louisville policeman, with tears rolling down his face, saluting the general. These people were standing up, screaming, hollering, and carrying on.

"So we proceed to the concert, where Lee Greenwood was going to sing 'God Bless the U.S.A.' to the general. Talk about a moment in your life. I will never forget that as long as I live. He came on stage and started singing that song, and I thought the roof was coming down in that place—19,000 people standing, screaming, waving, cheering. I've seen a lot of things in my long years, but I don't think I'll ever experience anything like that again in terms of reaction to a person [Schwarzkopf]."

Mangeot spoke in glowing terms of his personal experience with Schwarzkopf. "Great guy. One of the friendliest, nicest people I've ever met in my life. He loves to skeet shoot and fish. We set aside Friday so that we could do that for him.

"We got the Jefferson Gun Club to shut down and give us their facility. He had an enormous time skeet shooting. The first thing he said to me was, 'It's obvious you've never been in the military. You haven't hit anything yet.' I said, 'Thank you very much.'

"We left there and helicoptered over to [University of Louisville basketball coach] Denny Crum's lake to go fishing. Denny disappeared and gave us the place. The general got off the helicopter, and I was behind him. Maj. John Murty, his aide, was carrying this red telephone box, which he took wherever he went. All of a sudden the telephones went off. I said, 'Oh, my God.' I was looking for missile tracks in the sky. I was about to see a moment of history here. Major Murty handed the phone to the general. I was trying not to listen, but I was trying to listen.

"You know what I heard the general say? 'Well, how much does a refrigerator cost?' He had a tenant in an apartment building in Florida whose refrigerator went out. This tenant called the base, and they didn't know how else to get a hold of the general except on this hot line.

"Now can you imagine the Russians listening in to this hot line and saying, 'They got some kind of a new refrigerator weapon. What is the deal here?' It was awesome."

Mangeot said that it didn't cost the festival anything to bring in Schwarzkopf. "We paid for his hotel while he was here and escorted him around, but there was no fee involved," he said.

First Ruby Carried the Baby

Ruby said that in the early days he felt that the festival was his "baby." He added, "Nobody else would take the personal push in it to see that everything got done. *I* had to make it a success. I never had a failure in my thirty years, and I wasn't going to let this one fail."

When the festival was just crawling in those early years, it took men like Ruby and Wimberg, Caummisar and McGhee to keep it going. But Ruby is quick to downplay the role of the founders in the total scheme of things. "Too much attention, in my opinion, has been given to the founders," he said. "What we did was just a spit in the ocean, you could say, to what everybody else has done in this thing. It wasn't the festival as we know it today till years later when bigger men came in—bigger men with more money, more influence, more political influence and everything.

"Before, it was just four old men who sat down at a meeting and thought it up. Then it was up to me to carry the ball in the paper. And that's how it came about. I felt like as long as I had given birth to it, I had to wet-nurse it until it finally got on its feet."

Ruby is lavish in his praise of the work done by Mangeot, who had been with the festival since 1979. "Things just turned magical when Mangeot came in," he said. "I don't know of anybody in the world who could have done the job that he's done. And he does it so quietly. I never hear him go out and make loud speeches or anything. He's just in there working his tail off all the time. And he's got a staff that works like the devil."

And Then It Became Mangeot's Kid

Mangeot commented, "From a personal standpoint, this has been like growing a child. This has been—and I don't mean this selfishly because I didn't do it myself; a lot of people did it—but from a personal standpoint, this is like my kid. This is something I grew and had a great hand in growing. Had a lot of jobs in my life, made a lot of decisions, but nowhere like I've had to do here, where I really was able to get into it heart, soul, mind, and body and come up with things that work. It's been a great opportunity for me, and I love it."